WORKER SKILLS

AND

JOB REQUIREMENTS

ECONOMIC POLICY INSTITUTE

WORKER SKILLS

AND

JOB REQUIREMENTS

Is There a Mismatch?

◆

Michael J. Handel

ECONOMIC POLICY INSTITUTE

About the Author

Michael J. Handel is assistant professor of Sociology at the University of Wisconsin—Madison and a research associate at the Levy Economics Institute. He studies the growth of wage inequality in the United States and its relationship to technology, skills, and labor market institutions. He is currently conducting a national panel survey of wage and salary workers that address many of the issues raised in this study.

ECONOMIC POLICY INSTITUTE
1660 L Street, NW, Suite 1200
Washington, D.C. 20036

http://www.epinet.org

ISBN: 1-932066-16-0

Table of contents

Acknowledgments

I would like to thank Arne Kalleberg, Harry Holzer, Doug Harris, Gerald Handel, Ruth Handel, and the seminar participants at the Institute for Research on Poverty and the Department of Sociology, University of Wisconsin–Madison for their helpful comments on this work. I would also like to thank Lawrence Mishel and the Economic Policy Institute for their support of this work.

Introduction

There is a widespread belief that U.S. workers' education and skills are not adequate for the demands of jobs in the modern economy. Journalistic reports, employer surveys, popular and policy debates on school quality and education reform, sociological writings on the economy and the underclass, and economic research on the recent growth of wage inequality all suggest a mismatch between the skills workers possess and the skills jobs require, or what economists call an imbalance between supply and demand in the market for human capital. Many believe the imbalance will become even more serious because the pace of change in the labor market is accelerating and because the workplace is increasingly becoming a high-tech, service-oriented arena organized to involve greater employee participation in decision making (see Bresnahan et al. 2002 and also Smith 1997).

At an April 11, 2000 "National Skills Summit" sponsored by the Department of Labor, Federal Reserve Board Chairman Alan Greenspan remarked, "I see nothing to suggest that the trends toward...increased demand for conceptual skills in our workforce will end....Workers in many occupations are being asked to strengthen their cognitive skills." Such sentiments reflect those held by analysts who are concerned that a skills shortfall will harm the fortunes of those left behind, increase wage inequality, and limit economic growth.

Although many aspects of the skills mismatch issue seem self-evident to casual, and even some informed observers, a closer examination of its complexities reveals considerable ambiguity, requiring better data than are currently available to gain a clearer understanding of the issues. In fact, the very existence of a skills mismatch or skills shortage may be in doubt and is by no means as obvious as often asserted.

The somewhat limited and not completely consistent data currently available actually suggest that there is no evidence of declining skill levels in the U.S. workforce. Although growth in educational attainment decelerated in recent decades and cognitive test scores are not much higher than 30 years ago, skill demands have risen only gradually over time, with little direct evidence of any recent acceleration in skill demands linked to growth in wage inequality. Employers do complain about the skills of young workers and high-school-educated workers, but it is unclear whether they are dissatisfied mainly with workers' cognitive skills or rather with their effort and attitude. Also unclear is whether the decline in workforce quality is a transitory, life-cycle problem of young adults in general or a problem they will bear for all of their work lives, or whether it applies only to some fraction of disadvantaged minorities. Perhaps surprisingly, a lack of computer and other high-level skills are not oft-cited complaints, despite the frequent focus on computers as a principal source of skills change. Furthermore, the claims of accelerating demand for college graduates also do not seem to reflect employers' expressed needs.

This study aims to improve understanding of the issues involved in the skills mismatch debate. The first chapter provides some background and an overview of the skills mismatch issue. The following chapters review research on levels and trends in the skills workers possess, the skills employers demand, and the evidence for skill shortages or mismatches between the two. This tripartite structure is dictated by the nature of the data, which precludes a unified treatment of the question. There is limited reliable and representative data on workforce competencies, even less on job demands, and the evidence in each area is largely incommensurable. The need for a standard, common set of measures for worker skills and job skill requirements is the one key finding that emerges from this review of the existing data.

CHAPTER 1

Skills mismatch as a social problem

The term *skills mismatch* can describe situations in which workers' skills exceed or fall short of those employers seek. Indeed, social scientists' views on which situation applies have shifted from one position to the other in a relatively short time.

During the 1970s, many theorists believed workforce skill levels exceeded the levels that jobs could utilize. Credentialist theories in sociology argued that inflated hiring requirements led U.S. workers to obtain more education than they really needed for their jobs (Berg 1971; Collins 1979). Signaling and queuing theories in economics also cast a skeptical eye toward the meaningfulness of educational credentials; econometric studies of the falling differential between college- and high-school-educated workers led to the conclusion that Americans were overeducated (Freeman 1976). A prominent government report considered the dilemma of how to make work more satisfying when job complexity at all levels seemed to fall short of workers' rising education levels and aspirations for meaningful work (U.S. Department of Health, Education, and Welfare 1973). Deskilling theory claimed that the skill content of most jobs was actually declining, even as educational attainment continued to rise (Braverman 1973). Bowles and Gintis (1976) argued that schools mostly socialize students into the work norms appropriate for jobs at different levels of the class hierarchy, and this function of schooling plays a more important role in wage determination than its contribution to human capital formation.

In the 1980s and 1990s, with the exception of cultural capital theory in the sociology of education, academic and policy thinking shifted in the opposite direction, dramatically in some cases. More sociologists believed technology and sectoral shifts were increasing the relative number of high-skill jobs, as Daniel Bell's theory of a post-industrial or information economy claimed (Bell 1976; Form 1987; Attewell 1987; Wright and Martin 1987). William Julius Wilson, among others, argued that these changes contributed to the problems of the urban underclass by creating an increasing mismatch between the skills of minority workers and rising employer requirements (Wilson 1987 and 1996). Mainstream labor economists trying to explain the pronounced growth in overall wage inequality in the 1980s observed that the college premium rebounded from its record low point in the 1970s and reached record highs in the 1980s; they concluded that the growth in the demand for skill had outrun the supply in the general labor force (Katz and Murphy 1992). The skills glut somehow seemed to have turned rapidly into a severe shortage.

Separately, policy makers, employers, and the public expressed alarm at what they saw as declining academic skills among young people, reflected in falling test scores and the perceived decline of public schools. The United States seemed to rank relatively low in international test score comparisons while the Japanese, the United States' leading economic competitor, tended to rank high. The severe economic downturn in the early 1980s added urgency to calls for action (U.S. National Commission on Excellence in Education 1983). Government panels sought to clarify the skills that all workers needed (U.S. Department of Labor 1991) and authorized new programs to set national occupational skill standards and strengthen the connection between school and work, including borrowing aspects of the German apprenticeship system. Given the wave of plant closures in the recession of the early 1980s, previous concerns over trends in job satisfaction and the "blue-collar blues" seemed like luxuries when the very existence of whole segments of the job structure seemed at risk.

The most famous alarm came from *A Nation at Risk,* a report commissioned by the Department of Education:

> Our nation is at risk. Our once unchallenged preeminence in commerce, industry, science, and technological innovation is being overtaken by competitors throughout the world....The educational

foundations of our society are presently being eroded by a rising tide of mediocrity that threatens our very future as a nation and a people....If an unfriendly foreign power had attempted to impose on America the mediocre educational performance that exists today, we might well have viewed it as an act of war. As it stands, we have allowed this to happen to ourselves....We have, in effect, been committing an act of unthinking, unilateral educational disarmament. (National Commission on Excellence in Education 1983)

In addition to bemoaning declining high school and college entrance test scores and poor international test score rankings, the report expressed concern over increased use of remedial education, high rates of functional illiteracy, and the increased skill demands resulting from the spread of computers. Citing adult literacy surveys from the mid-1970s, the Secretary of Education testified before Congress that some 50% of adults were not "proficient in meeting the educational requirements of every day adult life" (Stedman and Kaestle 1991, 75 and 98f.), although if this were true it would apply mostly to people who completed their education prior to the ostensible decline in the school system. Poor performance by young adults on a literacy survey (1985) led the president of the Educational Testing Service (ETS) to worry about the large proportion of the population that "doesn't read well enough to cope with this technological society" (Reston 1986).

The concern is not restricted to the United States. Since roughly the early 1980s, Britain has been engaged in an almost identical debate filled with similar urgency and anguish, while Canada has experienced a somewhat muted version of the same (Payne 1999; Keep and Mayhew 1996; Krahn and Lowe 1998).

Interestingly, while education remains pilloried in political and public discourse, many of the economic problems that fueled concern in the 1980s and early 1990s diminished significantly thereafter, though no one attributes the economic improvements to schools, nor has the sense of urgency surrounding school quality and reform abated (Levin 1998a). Nevertheless, the preeminence of the U.S. economy is now unchallenged, economic growth was generally robust prior to the recent cyclical downturn, and the once-fearsome Japanese economy has been in the doldrums for a dozen years or so. Despite fears of a shortage of high-tech workers, the late 1990s boom was built largely around new computer technologies. Low unemployment in the 1990s boosted wages at the 10th percentile closer to the median, after significant declines in the 1980s, and overall wage inequality largely stopped rising.

The speed of this turnaround suggests that swings in macroeconomic forces had a far greater effect on the nation's fluctuating fortunes in the 1980s and 1990s than the modest trends in school quality or individual educational attainment. Indeed, the role reversal has been so complete that the Japanese are partly blaming their own education system for their recent economic difficulties and seeking to emulate aspects of the U.S. system, though the reforms are controversial in Japan (Ono 2002; French 2001). Recent research also attributes the growth of other newly industrializing East Asian countries more to high levels of investment and labor force growth than to their high test scores (Levin 1998a; Robinson 1998). Any skills mismatch explanation of U.S. wage inequality growth and poor economic performance for the 1980s has to account for the turnaround in the 1990s that seems largely independent of trends in the stock of worker skills. Levin (1998a) suggests that schools are simply scapegoats for poor economic performance, with the real sources laying elsewhere.

Indeed, labor economists in the segmented labor markets tradition argued that the real problem was not disappearing low-to-medium skill jobs *per se*, but rather the decline of unionized manufacturing jobs, which provided middle-class incomes for less-educated workers due to the institutional framework in which these jobs and workers were embedded. The lower-end service jobs that replaced them were less skilled and lower paid. The logic of secondary labor markets also intruded increasingly into the remaining jobs in the subordinate primary sector, as a result of deunionization, more competitive product markets, changing wage norms, the declining real value of the minimum wage, increasing use of contingent work, outsourcing, cheaper immigrant labor, and offshore production (Harrison and Bluestone 1988; Harrison 1994; Howell 1997; DiNardo et al. 1996). The highly restrictive macroeconomic policies designed to break inflation in the early 1980s also weakened labor's bargaining power by increasing unemployment to record postwar levels, which some argue was a far more important source of growing wage inequality than was computer technology or skills mismatch (Galbraith 1998).

From this point of view, identifying the problem as being one of workers' low skills diverted attention from the role of free-market government policies and management's shortcomings in product quality, capital investment, work organization, and worker training (Levin 1998a; Mishel and Teixeira 1991). It is changes in the quality of jobs, not a shortage of human capital, that explains wage inequality growth. From a sociological perspective, the skills mismatch discourse can be seen as blaming those who bear the brunt of low-road management strategies for their straits. In its more extreme forms, this discourse creates a kind of "moral panic" that generates a level of concern over skills disproportionate to that warranted by sober assessment of the evidence (Goode and Ben-Yehuda 1994).

Closer inspection of the skills mismatch thesis confirms it has significant problems or gaps, both conceptual and empirical. Specifically, proponents of the skills mismatch thesis have not been clear about the subgroups, particular skills, precise trends, and underlying causes they consider to be the main problems. Consequently, they offer disparate diagnoses, and the evidence for many of these diagnoses is weak. The different voices in the skills mismatch discussion can appear like the proverbial blind men who perceive, or misperceive, different parts of the same elephant. **Table 1** summarizes some of the unresolved issues, which are threaded through this study and explained briefly below.

Which groups and what skills or other labor force characteristics are at issue?

Different skills mismatch theories identify different groups as a cause for concern—cohorts educated since the 1960s, young workers, older workers, disadvantaged minorities, job-seekers with a high school education or less, and even college-educated workers lacking technical backgrounds.

Correspondingly, the different theories identify different skills or other labor force characteristics in short supply—8th or 10th grade-level reading, writing, and math skills; college-level cognitive skills;

TABLE 1   Unresolved issues in the skills mismatch literature

Who lacks necessary skills?
- Recent cohorts
- Young workers
- Older workers
- Workers with a high school degree or less
- Disadvantaged minorities
- College-educated workers lacking strong math, science, or other technical training

What specific skills or qualities are in short supply?
- Basic or intermediate reading, writing, and math skills
- Advanced cognitive/intellectual skills
- "Problem-solving" skills
- Technology competencies
- Interpersonal ("soft") skills
- Attitudes and work ethic, effort, diligence, commitment, sense of responsibility, respect for authority

How is any trend best characterized?
- Absolute decline in the supply of skills
- Decelerating growth in the supply of skills
- Accelerating growth in the demand for skills

What is responsible for any shortage?
- Employer changes (technology, organizational change)
- Workforce quality and characteristics:
  ° Failing schools
  ° Underclass conditions
  ° Demographic trends in cohort sizes and college enrollment rates

generally unspecified "problem-solving" abilities; computer skills; social or interpersonal skills, such as teamwork or customer service; or work-related attitudes, such as motivation, effort, and willingness to follow directions, which strictly speaking are not skills at all.

One of the most prominent versions of the skills mismatch thesis, emanating from the school failure literature, focuses on basic or intermediate (8th-10th grade) skills deficits among young people and implies the problem lies with those educated since the 1960s, when test scores fell and school quality is believed to have declined. It should be noted that arguing that declining school quality permanently affects student outcomes frames the argument in terms of educational cohorts; that is, poorer skills are presumably persistent characteristics of affected groups that should be apparent in comparisons between adults educated before and after the 1960s.

However, the literature also alleges another problem related to personality, some of which are not skills strictly speaking. These include inadequate interpersonal and teamwork skills ("soft skills"), respect for authority and other attitudinal or demeanor issues, and related problems with work motivation, effort, and sense of responsibility (Moss and Tilly 2001, 44f. and p. 60). The usually vague concern regarding "problem-solving" skills seems to fall on both sides of this divide; employers seem to use this term to express dissatisfaction with both workers' cognitive skills and their perceived lack of interest in exercising them.

Complaints about social skills and motivation suggest that what is often perceived as a cohort effect may be an age effect. Recent cohorts may pass through a phase of early adulthood characterized by low effort and weak attachment to career employment, reinforced by a scarcity of jobs offering career opportunities. As workers age and shoulder more adult responsibilities, they grow out of casual work attitudes and adjust to—or are socialized into—the workplace norms of the jobs they consider worth keeping, and they compensate for any modest cognitive skill deficits through on-the-job experience and situated learning (Scribner 1986).

Casual support for this view comes from the fact that complaints regarding younger workers have persisted for more than 20 years, but similar complaints regarding older workers do not seem to have emerged as the earlier cohorts aged; complaints persistently refer to age groups rather than cohorts. Indeed, Scholastic Aptitude/Assessment Test (SAT) and other test scores stopped declining or started rising after 1980, yet the complaints about young workers, usually undifferentiated according to cognitive skills and personality characteristics, persist (*Economic Report of the President* 2000, p. 148). Cohorts cited by *A Nation at Risk* are now middle aged and are not only seldom the subject of the blanket complaints directed at youth but are among those who themselves complain about declining skills among young people, even though middle-aged cohorts scored lower than younger ones. This should be cause for doubt as to whether the problem is really cognitive skills rather than work-related attitudes.

If the problem is attitudes, then employers may face a chronic problem with young workers, but the problem for each cohort is likely to be transient. The overall labor force does not face a progressive problem in this case because each cohort can be expected to age out of its phase of weak attachment to career goals.

Insofar as one believes the new economy places a premium on computer or similar technology-related competencies, one might expect that premium to favor younger workers over older ones, who have greater potential difficulty assimilating new skills and face issues of skill obsolescence and retraining (Friedberg 2001; U.S. Congress Office of Technology Assessment 1990, p. 254; Kelley and Charness 1995; Westerman et al. 1995).

Until this point, this discussion of the skills mismatch thesis has been framed in terms of the workforce overall, but much of the mismatch theory focuses on workers with a high school degree or less or—an even narrower group—less-educated, disadvantaged minorities. If a skills mismatch exists, but only for these groups, this clearly affects the magnitude of the problem and should be distinguished from the idea that schools are failing to impart sufficient skills more generally.

Likewise, debates over alleged declines in the quality of higher education or inadequate numbers of college graduates are very different from concerns that not enough high school graduates have 10th-grade reading and math skills (Murnane and Levy 1996). Public controversy over recentering SAT scores (Winerip 1994), grade inflation in higher education (Rothstein 2001), stagnation or decline in the number of students receiving bachelor's degrees in math, science, and engineering (National Research Council 2001), and the attention given by labor economists to the declining rates of college attendance in general (Card and Lemieux 2001) are all quite distinct from concerns over skills at the lower end of the distribution. But these disparate issues are often folded into the same discussion of skills adequacy.

In sum, existing notions of a skills mismatch are a confused jumble of different ideas, "sketchy, vague, and diverse if not internally conflicting," to borrow a phrase (Cain 1976, p. 1221). A satisfying skills mismatch argument ultimately must specify whether the problem is a shortage of cognitive skills or a surplus of youthful attitudes, not enough workers with 10th-grade reading and math skills or too few high-powered "symbolic analysts" (Reich 1991), and it must specify whether the problem is the quality of public school students generally or just high school dropouts and certain disadvantaged groups.

What is the nature of skill trends?

A final ambiguity in the skills mismatch literature is the nature of skill trends. Different proponents of the skills mismatch thesis argue there is an *absolute decline* in skills across cohorts or other large subgroups, *slowing growth* in the supply of human capital, or *accelerating growth* in demand for human capital. Those concerned with education and schools are more likely to speak in terms of absolute decline. Labor economists researching inequality are still undecided as to whether slowing growth in supply or acceleration in demand is more significant (Katz and Murphy 1992; Autor et al. 1998; Gottschalk and Smeeding 1997; Card and Lemieux 2001).

The differences have clear implications for the evidence that one considers and one's understanding of the problem. Absolute declines or slower growth in the supply of workers' human capital point to problems with the education system and worker behavior, with root causes such as failing schools, underclass conditions, and falling rates of college enrollment. In contrast, accelerating demand for human capital suggests employer-side changes, such as the spread of computer technology or employee participation, are responsible for the skills mismatch. The evidence relating to each kind of explanation is quite distinct.

As it happens, there is little compelling evidence that either workers' skills or employers' demands for human capital have changed in ways that would support simple notions of a skills mismatch. With the preceding considerations in mind, the next chapter reviews the evidence on workers' skills, employers' needs, and possible mismatches.

CHAPTER 2

Workers' skills:
Education and test scores

Trends and cross-sectional evidence in the United States

The most frequently used and available measure of workers' skills is the quantity of workers' education, measured in years of schooling or degree attained, but recent concern has also focused on educational quality, as measured by test score trends.

Educational attainment

If quantity of education is the measure, then today's workforce is considerably more skilled than in the past. In 1964, before the perceived deterioration of public education, 47% of all Americans were high school dropouts, as were 31% of young people aged 24 to 29, who would have graduated between 1953 and 1958. In contrast, only 13% of all Americans and those age 24 to 29 were dropouts in 1997 (author's calculations based on March Current Population Survey). Clearly, viewing the period prior to the late 1960s as a golden age for either worker skills or the public education system is as much an exercise in nostalgia as a balanced assessment.

The rate of growth in educational attainment since the 1960s has varied and depends on the measure (for example, mean years of education versus categories of attainment) and on whether all workers or only younger workers are considered. In general, March Current Population Survey (CPS) data for the 1960s to 1990s indicate that attainment for the entire population grew most rapidly through the mid-1970s, decelerated somewhat between 1975 and 1982 and between 1982 and 1991, and decelerated somewhat further in the 1990s. Attainment among those age 24 to 29 rose most rapidly between 1965 and 1975, due to both rapidly declining high school dropout rates and rising college attendance rates, boosted in part and temporarily by Vietnam draft deferments. For young workers the trend in attainment was largely flat between 1975 and 1990 and turned up somewhat between 1990 and 1997, a period when economic conditions improved, though concern over education remained intense. Inequality in educational attainment as measured by the coefficient of variation declined 25-30%, both for all workers and for young workers between 1962 and 1982, then remained flat (author's calculations).

If educational attainment is the measure of skill, then the workforce today is more skilled than ever, though improvement was flat for young workers when concern over both education and the economy was great (1975-90). Of course, if employers' requirements have risen faster than trends in attainment, then stability or even growth in educational attainment may be insufficient to prevent skills shortages and the bidding up of wages for the more educated, but this is not evidence of an absolute decline either in human capital stocks or school performance.

Test scores

Because of concern over variations in the quality of schooling and the coarseness of educational categories, test scores have been used as another, arguably more precise measure of cognitive skills, though such data are not plentiful, especially if one wants extended time series with large, representative samples.

Economists of education and policy analysts are especially likely to focus on public school test scores and recommend large-scale overhaul of public education through high-stakes testing and school vouchers as a way to enhance the skills of the U.S. workforce, citing trends in educational wage differentials described by labor economists.

Interestingly, most labor economists who study the growth in wage inequality do not view declining educational quality or test scores as the main problem, partly because older as well as younger high school graduates suffered wage declines even though they completed their education prior to the 1960s. Most labor economists see the issue of wage inequality mainly in terms of declining growth in the quantity (years) of education attained, particularly declining growth in the number of college graduates (for example, Katz and Murphy 1992; Danziger and Gottschalk 1995, 134f.; Card and Lemieux 2001; but see Bishop 1989, p. 188; Bishop 1991; and Murnane et al. 1995).

Intelligence tests. Intelligence or IQ tests show large gains for Americans throughout this century, including every postwar decade for samples as recent as 1995, the most current, and there is no obvious recent change in the rate of growth (Flynn 1998, p. 27 and 35ff.). The gains in the United States and other industrialized countries are so large that intense controversy persists over whether they can be taken at face value because they imply either abnormally low intelligence in test takers of the early 20th century or very high rates of giftedness today, depending on which sample is taken as the standard. Even if cohort gains in mean IQ test scores do not signify commensurate gains in actual intelligence, they do not suggest declines. The struggle in explaining IQ trends is discovering the reason for their unexpected and robust growth.

Since 1974 the General Social Survey has administered a 10-word vocabulary test selected from a larger intelligence test. This is the fullest time series for a representative sample of Americans, but its brevity and relatively small sample size introduce more measurement error and sampling variance than is ideal. The mean for all workers does seem to have declined erratically by as much as 0.17 standard deviations between the late 1970s and late 1980s, but it then regained its former level in the 1990s (Handel 2000). While there has been strong disagreement over whether scores declined for younger cohorts (Alwin 1991; Wilson and Gove 1999a, 1999b; Glenn 1999; Alwin and McCammon 1999), there are much better trend data on cognitive test scores of young people in particular, described below.

College entrance exams. One of the most frequently cited sources of information are college entrance exams, such as the SAT, whose decline beginning in the mid-1960s initiated the recent concern over the state of public education in the United States. However, less widely reported is that math SAT scores started rising around 1980 and exceeded 1971 levels by the mid-1990s, despite the growing share of high school students taking the exam, though verbal scores did not recover. In contrast, trends for the rival American College Test (ACT) show English scores exceeding earlier levels in recent years and the rebound in math not fully offsetting the earlier decline (*Economic Report of the President* 2000, p. 148; Boesel and Fredland 1999, p. 72). The tests differ in their emphasis and the pool of students taking them, but it is not obvious why trends differ across the two tests. Contrary to popular perception, the

SAT and ACT test score declines are highly cohort-specific; even adjusted for recentering, the decline in SAT test scores ceased (verbal) or reversed (math) 20 years ago. Other tests confirm that any downward trend in test scores was restricted to the 1960s and 1970s (Koretz 1986, 1992).

However, a problem with college entrance exams is that the population of test-takers is not random. The composition and percentage of high school students who self-select into the test pool has changed so much over time that some observers believe no credible conclusions can be drawn from this data (Hauser 1998, p. 224). Others argue that a genuine decline can be inferred at least for the early 1970s. During this period, scores continued to fall even though the selectivity of the pool of test-takers likely increased because fewer high school students applied to college after the end of Vietnam draft deferments for college students (Koretz 1992). This conclusion is clouded by the fact that the shorter, Preliminary Scholastic Aptitude Test (PSAT) has been normed on representative samples of high school juniors and apparently shows no trend in either the mean or interquartile range since the early 1960s, and the variance seems to have declined during this period (Williams and Ceci 1997). However, some critics detect an upward drift in the scaling of PSAT scores over time that masks declining performance (Jones 1981).

National Assessment of Educational Progress (NAEP). The best time series of inter-cohort data is the U.S. Department of Education's National Assessment of Educational Progress (NAEP), sometimes called the Nation's Report Card, which has a continuous series of reading and math scores for representative samples of 17-year olds since the early 1970s. The test instrument has remained relatively unchanged in the last 30 years. Reading scores did not change significantly between 1971 and 1999, though the general direction of change was upward, in contrast to SAT scores. Math scores fell approximately 0.18 standard deviations between 1973 and 1982, and then rose almost continuously, exceeding the 1973 level by 0.13 standard deviations in 1999 (Campbell et al. 2000; Peterson 2003). Even critics of American educational performance acknowledge changes of this magnitude are not large (Peterson 2003, p. 42).

Peterson notes that because the NAEP depends on voluntary compliance on the part of schools and students and is a low-stakes test, it is possible that mean scores stopped falling because of declining participation rates among students who might receive low scores had they took the test (2003, p. 48ff.). However, NAEP mean scores are adjusted for differences in participation rates, and in any case participation rates did not decline for the reading test prior to 1999, nor for the math test between 1978 and 1996 (Campbell et al. 2000; p. 88f.). The mean scores show no breaks in the other years, and trends in reading scores at the 5th and 10th percentiles also do not suggest increased exclusion of low-scoring students over time, though similar figures for the math tests were not available in the sources consulted (U.S. Department of Education 2001, Table 113).

The stability or gain in mean scores was not accompanied by increased test score inequality. Overall test score inequality (interquartile range) for both math and reading has declined by roughly 6% since the 1970s, due mostly to gains in the lower percentiles—contradicting the perception that the lower part of the distribution is losing ground (Campbell et al. 2000, p. 9ff.). Math and reading scores among black Americans rose and closed roughly half of the black/white gap during the 1980s, also contradicting popular perceptions, before losing some ground in the 1990s—a development still poorly understood (Campbell et al. 2000, p. 36ff.).

The dominant impression given by NAEP scores is their stability. If employer skill demands are rising, then this relative stability may be cause for concern, but it is a far cry from the common rhetoric of *declining* student achievement and failing schools.

Table 2 summarizes the basic trends for the intelligence tests, college entrance exams, and the NAEP for the 1970s through the present. The table shows clearly the improvement in almost all series since the 1970s and the higher scores in recent years compared to the earliest years of the various time series. Table 2 also shows the different behavior of verbal and math scores over the period, depending on whether one looks at the SAT or ACT and on how both sets of results differ from the trend in intelligence test scores. The table's descriptions of the changes in NAEP reading scores should not be given great weight because none of the scores differ significantly from the mean for 1999—that is to say, the trend for reading scores over the entire period is basically flat (Campbell et al. 2000, p. xi).

Because raw scores mean little to policy makers and the public, the NAEP scale was also divided into five performance categories that, in

TABLE 2   Summary of test score trends

Test	1970s	1980s	1990s	1990s-1970s *
WAIS (1970-2000)	Rising	Rising	Rising	Higher
SAT (1971-96)				
Verbal	Falling	Falling	Rising	Lower
Math	Falling	Rising	Rising	Higher
ACT (1970-95)				
English	Falling	Rising	Rising	Higher
Math	Falling	Rising	Rising	Lower
NAEP				
Reading (1971-99)	Stable	Rising	Falling	Higher
Math (1973-99)	Falling	Rising	Rising	Higher

Note:
WAIS=Wechsler Adult Intelligence Scale (Flynn 1998: 37)
SAT=Scholastic Aptitude/Assessment Test (1971-96) (Economic Report of the President 2000: 148; Koretz 1986: 38; Peterson 2003: 49)
ACT=American College Test (1970-1995) (Boesel and Fredland 1999: 72)
NAEP=National Assessment of Educational Progress (Campbell et al. 2000: xi). None of the changes in the NAEP *reading* scores are large enough to reach statistical significance.

* This column indicates whether the test score at the end of each series is higher or lower than the score at the beginning of the series.

principle, offer some concrete indication of the tasks that students with different scores can perform. Using this yardstick, reading test scores indicate that roughly 80% of 17-year olds in the years between 1971 and 1999 can "organize the information they find in relatively lengthy passages and can recognize paraphrases of what they have read…make inferences and reach generalizations about main ideas and author's purpose from passages dealing with literature, science, and social studies." For math, approximately 95% of 17-year olds in the years between 1978 and 1999 can "apply whole number addition and subtraction skills to one-step word problems and money situations….find the product of a two-digit and one-digit number….[and] compare information from graphs and charts," while more than 55% performed at least well enough to qualify for the rather more heterogeneous category that included the ability to solve problems with decimals, manipulate simple fractions and percents, "identify geometric figures, measure lengths and angles," and begin to work with exponents and square roots (Campbell et al. 2000, p. 16ff.).

Although the generally small proportions scoring at the highest NAEP performance level often receives great attention, it seems that the number of people able to perform at this level does grow as people age. In one sample of test takers age 21 to 25, 21% scored in the highest performance level on a set of NAEP reading exercises (Kirsch and Jungeblut 1986, p. 38), compared to 5% for members of the same cohort when they were aged 17 (Campbell et al. 2000, p. 21). It is not clear how much of this improvement is due solely to the greater education of the older sample, as opposed to increased exposure to reading materials in work and non-work contexts over time. However, the evidence suggests that the NAEP scores of 17-year olds cannot be taken at face value as measures of young adult competencies.

Adult reading and math scores. There is much less complete or representative information on adult reading and math skills over time. A review of several tests administered to large, representative samples of adults in the 1970s and early 1980s concluded that approximately 20% of the adult population had serious difficulties with common reading tasks and another 10% had better but still marginal functional literacy skills (Stedman and Kaestle 1991, p. 109). The different tests are not comparable, making trend analyses impossible, but most samples included only a small proportion of adults who completed their education in the late 1960s-70s, when educational quality is believed to have declined. Therefore, this figure might be taken as an informal estimate of the low-skilled share of the labor force during the most prosperous years of the old economy, and an informal baseline against which more recent estimates may be evaluated.

The richest source of data is the cross-sectional National Adult Literacy Survey (NALS) (1992), sponsored by the U.S. Department of Education and developed by the Educational Testing Service (ETS), which also writes the SAT. Consisting of questions based on real-world situations that individuals would encounter in everyday life and work, the NALS was administered to a large, nationally representative sample of adults. Its results are highly informative, though it should be noted that when one sample of test takers completed a battery of both NAEP- and NALS-style reading exercises, the correlation between scores on the two tests was a relatively moderate 0.58, suggesting that a construct like reading literacy or cognitive ability is complex and multidimensional (Kirsch and Jungeblut 1986, p. 41).

The NALS measured skills in dealing with prose (such as newspaper articles or product instructions), documents (payroll forms, bus schedules, graphs, and so on), and quantitative materials (calculating a tip, balancing a checkbook, determining interest from a loan advertisement). Since the scores on the three scales tend to be so similar, **Table 3** reports the simple average across the scales for all adults and various subgroups (column 1) and the difference between subgroup means and the overall mean in standard deviation units (column 2). The NALS also reported results in terms of discrete performance levels (column 3), defined by various cut-points to facilitate interpretability for policy makers and the public.

The most widely reported result was the large number of Americans (22%) in the lowest literacy level, Level 1 (column 3). Less noticed was that the implications for the quality of the labor force were not clear-cut. A third of those scoring in Level 1 were over 65 years old, many of whom are retired people with less education than younger adults and depressed cognitive functioning due to aging. Likewise, roughly a quarter were foreign-born, many with limited English skills and limited schooling in their native countries. Some two-thirds did not finish high school, and a third did not complete more than 8th grade. A quarter also reported a disability that prevented them from participating fully in work, and nearly a fifth reported impaired vision (Kirsch et al. 1993, p. 16ff.).

The percentage of full-time workers in Level 1 (13%) is considerably lower than in the population as a whole. This figure has been used to suggest that the labor market filters out many low-scoring individuals, but clearly many Americans in the overall population performing at Level 1 are out of the labor market for reasons unrelated to low skills, such as age or physical disability. In addition, many in Level 1 who are employed have been drawn into the U.S. labor market from abroad, often to work for employers happy to trade off these workers' lower English literacy skills for the low pay they will accept. Clearly, the reported numbers in Level 1 cannot be used in a straightforward manner to draw conclusions about the number of native-born potential job seekers who are hard to employ because of low skills. Nor can one draw

TABLE 3   National Adult Literacy (NALS) test scores, 1992

	Mean	SD units	Percentage (employed full time)
All	270		
Level 1 (0-225)			22.0 (13.0)
Level 2 (226-275)			26.7 (24.3)
Level 3 (276-325)			31.3 (35.3)
Level 4 (326-375)			16.3 (22.3)
Level 5 (376-500)			3.3 (5.0)
In labor force	283	0.20	
Employed full time	287	0.27	
Unemployed	258	-0.19	
Not in labor force	241	-0.45	
Employed full time			
<= 1.25 poverty level	251	-0.30	
Not poor	298	0.44	
Out of labor force			
<= 1.25 poverty level	213	-0.89	
Not poor	265	-0.08	
Some high school	228	-0.66	
GED	267	-0.05	
High school	268	-0.03	
2-year college degree	305	0.55	
Bachelors	319	0.77	
Postgraduate	332	0.97	
Manager/prof'l/technical	320	0.78	
Clerical/sales	291	0.33	
Craft	267	-0.05	
Operator/laborer	251	-0.30	
Services	262	-0.13	
Age (high school dates)			
19-24 (1986-1991)	279	0.14	
25-39 (1971-1985)	283	0.20	
40-54 (1956-1970)	283	0.20	
55-64 (1946-1955)	257	-0.20	
65+ (<= 1945)	225	-0.70	
White	284	0.22	
Black	230	-0.63	

Note: All values are simple means of prose, document, and literacy scores. Values in column 2 subtract the overall mean from values in column 1 and divide by the full sample estimate of standard deviation of 64 (Devroye and Freeman 2001). Some occupational means are weighted averages of means for narrower occupational groups.   Unless otherwise noted, figures refer to all Americans, not simply workers. Source: Kirsch et al. (1993: 17, 26, 31, 33) and Sum (1999: 24, 32ff., 62, 76ff.)

conclusions about the adequacy of American schools in equipping the future workforce with skills. Indeed, educational professionals and researchers using the NALS complain that the demographic heterogeneity within Level 1 limits the usefulness of the category (U.S. Department of Education 1998).

Nevertheless, column 2 from Table 3 indicates that the unemployed and working poor do have below-average scores. Approximately 15-20% of those in Levels 1 and 2 were unemployed in 1992, compared to 8% in Level 3, 5% in Levels 4 and 5, and a national average of 7.4% (Sum 1999, pp. 39, 45). For the sake of completeness, Table 3 also includes scores for those out of the labor force, but these scores cannot be taken at face value because the NALS reports did not exclude older and disabled Americans. These groups are disproportionately lower scoring but not really labor market dropouts, so they should be excluded from any analysis of a possible skills mismatch.

Not surprisingly, there are large test score gaps between high school dropouts and high school graduates, and between high school graduates and those with some college education. However, there is no difference between GED holders and high school graduates. Differences in scores by level of post-secondary schooling are also significant but more incremental. Occupational differences are also in the expected direction and they parallel the results by education level.

Contrary to popular preconceptions, age is negatively associated with test scores, even for those under 65, lending no support to the idea that younger Americans have poorer literacy skills than older Americans. Those aged 55-64, who would have graduated high school in the allegedly golden years of American education (1946-55), clearly have lower scores than more recent cohorts, who supposedly bear the effects of less-rigorous schooling. Significantly fewer Americans in the older group actually finished high school, but a significant age gap remains even after controlling for educational attainment (Smith 1995, p. 214; Freeman and Schettkat 2001; OECD and Statistics Canada 2000, p. 147f.). Some unknown portion of the gap may reflect aging effects, just as the scores for the youngest group will likely improve as a function of increased education and experience, which the NAEP reading results comparisons suggest. Nevertheless, from available data one finds no evidence that more recent cohorts have lower cognitive skills than older cohorts; indeed, the reverse seems true. If poor schooling was a problem for members of more recent cohorts, they had overcome any deficit by the time the NALS was administered.

As with other tests, the gap between racial and ethnic groups is large, and roughly three-quarters of the gap remains even when published tabulations compare scores within education groups, though there are no formal analyses controlling for age, family background, or quality of schooling (Kirsch et al. 1993, p. 35). However, consistent with the narrowing of the gap between black and white scores on the NAEP, the race gap is narrower for younger adults; in 1992, the gap for those age 19-24 was roughly a third less than for those age 40-54, which is consistent with the view that racial disparities are declining over time (Kirsch et al. 1993, p. 39).

The meaning of test scores in the context of skills mismatch debates

The meaning of test scores such as the NAEP and NALS is much debated, and these debates are important for understanding the value and limitations of test scores in the skills mismatch debate. The most prominent debate involves skeptics who say the tests underestimate the real-world skills of minorities and low-scoring individuals and that they show bias, either in their content or in how they are used in employee selection (Hartigan and Wigdor 1989; Sticht 1992; Jencks 1998). The other side of this debate includes those in education, industrial/organizational psychology, and traditional intelligence psychology who argue that test scores are among the strongest predictors of outcomes, including job performance, which is usually measured by supervisor ratings but sometimes by physical productivity or sales records (Hunter and Schmidt 1998; Gottfredson 1997).

Testing advocates argue that those who score higher perform many jobs faster and more accurately, require shorter training and less assistance from supervisors and coworkers, and can generalize their knowledge better to unfamiliar situations than can lower-scoring workers. However, they acknowledge that test scores account for a modest proportion of overall variance in job performance and wages, that personality traits and work attitudes are also important predictors of job performance, and that the strength of association between test score and job performance is smaller for less complex jobs (Hunter and Schmidt 1998; Gottfredson 1997).

Other debates center around the value of using tests as measures of school productivity or as high school graduation requirements—so-called "high stakes testing" (Koretz 2000).

Many of these debates involve the meaning of test score rankings of individuals or their value in benchmarking school quality. However, less noticed are the problems involved in drawing conclusions about the absolute level of real world proficiencies from test scores or the discrete performance categories constructed for them. As the Education Secretary's comments in the previous chapter illustrate, there is a strong impulse to use test scores to infer absolute levels of cognitive skills, that is, the specific tasks individuals can or cannot perform outside the test situation and their match with the economy's skill requirements, rather than seeing test scores merely as measures of relative rank. In the language of test psychology, the tests are treated as criterion-referenced rather than norm-referenced, assuming an easy way to link test scores with real-world proficiencies that can then be compared to the skills demanded by employers. In fact, there are good reasons to believe test scores do not map easily into conclusions regarding what people can and cannot do outside the test situation. (Chapter 3 discusses the state of data on employers' skill demands.)

Because the raw scores are uninterpretable by themselves, the discrete performance categories are central to drawing a connection between test scores and real-world proficiencies, but they have a number of problems. One obvious problem is that any division of a continuous scale into discrete categories is arbitrary and will give a misleading impression of the abilities of those near the cut points.

More seriously, the performance levels themselves have significant reliability and validity problems, at least for the NAEP. The testing organization constructs performance categories to assist interpretation by those outside the professional testing community. This requires assigning test questions to the different performance levels and then calculating the performance levels of test takers based on their probability of answering correctly the questions at that level of difficulty. Along with the results, the NAEP releases sample items and category descriptions intended to illustrate and explain the meaning of the different performance levels.

Evaluators have recommended that the reporting of results by performance levels be discontinued because raters' assignment of test items to performance levels is unreliable, the proportion of students answering the publicly released sample items correctly can diverge significantly from the proportion classified in the performance level that the items illustrate, and the competency descriptions attached to the levels tend to give a lower impression of students' abilities than warranted by their scores on other tests (Pellegrino et al. 1999, p. 166f.; Linn et al. 1996, p. 27; Campbell et al. 2000, p. 17f., 93f.).

While the NALS has not received the same scrutiny, sample items and their assigned performance levels also suggest that individuals' real-world capabilities would be underestimated if their performance on NALS tasks were interpreted literally as reflecting the tasks they could and could not perform in their daily lives (such as calculating a tip, reading a bus schedule, or understanding a news article) (Sum 1999, p. 277ff.).

In addition, respondents' self-reports of their literacy practices and competencies suggest significantly more advanced skills than would be expected on the basis of their scores. Some 64% to 75% of those in the NALS Level 1 said they read and write English "well" or "very well," and only 14% to 25% reported receiving help from others in performing everyday reading, writing, and math tasks (Kirsch et al. 1993, p. 20ff.).

The low levels of reported problems may reflect distorted self-perceptions or a match between low-skilled workers and low-skilled (and low-paying) jobs, but it is also possible that the test is in some respects, and for some people, a misleading measure of their abilities outside the test situation. For example, roughly 35% in Level 1 reported reading a newspaper daily, which—while significantly below the 50-60% reporting daily newspaper reading for the other levels—is not necessarily in line with descriptions of Level 1 competencies (Kirsch et al. 1993, p. 55).

Such apparent discrepancies between the description of the performance levels and individuals' real-world capabilities should not be entirely unexpected. For both the NAEP and NALS, assignment to performance levels signifies a high probability of correctly answering items at the assigned level, but the choice of a probability criterion that determines the level assignment is itself arbitrary and the subject of controversy. The NAEP math test assigns test-takers' scores to performance levels based on a 65% probability of answering correctly the items classified at that level, while the reading test uses an 80% criterion (Campbell et al. 2000, p. 93). The NALS uses an 80% criterion for all scales. By contrast, the Third International Mathematics and Science Study, a widely reported international test of student achievement, uses 65%, the OECD-sponsored Program for International Student Assessment uses 62%, and the Comprehensive Adult Student Assessment System (a widely used test for adult education approved by the Department of Education) uses a criterion of 50% (U.S. Department of Education 1998, p. 28; OECD 2001, p. 15). Likewise, the grade level of reading materials has been defined as the grade at which the average student can understand 75% of the material, but other standards are also used (Stedman and Kaestle 1991, p. 113, 117f.).

Using different thresholds will result in classifying people into different literacy categories purely as a function of the criteria used to define proficiency, yet there seems to be no strong conceptual or theoretical reason for choosing one standard over another, as the different tests illustrate. The original project manager for the NALS at the National Center for Educational Statistics (NCES) in the Department of Education argued recently that a 50% criterion was more reasonable than the original 80%, and that the former should replace the latter as the basis for calculating assignment to levels. This change would cut the proportion classified in Level 1 by more than half. The NALS study director at the Educational Testing Service strenuously objected to the alternative standard (Mathews 2001). They did not disagree over the raw scoring procedures or individual rankings of test takers, but how scores should be mapped into specific performance categories, which is the relevant issue for anyone wanting to know the kinds of tasks people can perform and whether they match job skill requirements.

Despite disagreements over specific criteria, everyone agrees that assignment to a given performance level does not signify the test-taker is unable to perform tasks characteristic of higher levels, but rather that he or she has a lower probability of doing so. For example, individuals with NALS scores of 250, in the middle of Level 2 and just below the average for high school graduates, have roughly a 50% probability of performing tasks at Level 3 (where scores for two-year college grads cluster) and a 30% probability of performing tasks at Level 4 (which Table 3 suggests is above average for those with at least a bachelor's degree) (Sum 1999, p.

305ff.). The same principle applies to those scoring at other levels on the NALS and NAEP.

Even these figures do not provide a concrete indication of how easily individuals could acquire greater skills through increased training and experience if their jobs were to require them. Nor does it reflect the extent to which current scores might be depressed for some people as a result of their working in jobs that do not require extensive literacy and which contribute to the atrophy of cognitive skills (Schooler 1998). Human capital theory recognizes this endogeneity problem implicitly in its concept of skill depreciation to describe the loss of valuable skills as a result of disuse.

The fact that individuals who score at one performance level are able to perform tasks at a higher level greatly complicates efforts to draw specific or strong conclusions about absolute skill levels in the labor force. Most popular reports of test results ignore this fact. One analysis of media reports on the NAEP criticized them for using simplistic descriptions of the performance levels and for tending to "misrepresent student achievement as discontinuous—students either can or cannot do what is in the descriptions of the levels. Both of these tendencies are illustrated, for example, by a statement that students at Level 200 'know how to add'" (Linn et al. 1996, p. 26).

As another example, *Education Week*, reporting on the large proportion of test takers in NALS Levels 1 and 2, declared, "Nearly half of all adult Americans cannot read, write, and calculate well enough to function fully in today's society" (quoted in U.S. Department of Education 2000, p. 23). A well-known education writer concluded from reports based on an earlier, young-adult version of the NALS that "80% can't calculate a tip in a restaurant or figure out which bus will get them home by using a schedule that is no more difficult than the ones most of us decipher every day" (Kozol 1986). These do not seem to be plausible conclusions.

These often-repeated conclusions suggest not only that the vast majority of Americans are unfit for even moderately skilled jobs, but that they might even have trouble finding their way to work, even though millions of Americans—disproportionately lower-income and likely lower-scoring—take public transportation every day. Clearly, the issue of measuring skill levels in an absolute sense is not resolved by the use of performance levels and accompanying sample test questions.

The problems associated with inferring real-world cognitive skills from test performance point to other limitations of such tests. The tests are intended as measures of functional literacy, but completing paper-and-pencil exercises in a solitary context are not a realistic model of how most people actually function. In everyday life, people interact with others and can ask them for clarification or assistance when they find something confusing, while this is not permitted in most test situations. Taken too far, the need for help from others might make someone unsuitable for a given job, but tests that prohibit collaboration altogether are likely to give an unrealistically low estimate of people's actual functional abilities. In addition, the test situation is itself a social situation in which not everyone feels equally at home. People who were uncomfortable in school and with the cultural style associated with school, including abstract reasoning tasks in formal contexts, also perform less well on the artificial problems posed by school-like tests, as compared to analogous tasks in their actual work life (Schooler 1998, p. 70).

This distinction between academic or test-taking skills and real-world competencies is reflected in an alternative conception of skills, often known as *situated cognition* or *practical intelligence*. Traditional testing and intelligence psychology believe that individual testing with pre-structured, often abstract tasks in a formal setting generally provides the best measure of cognitive skill. The alternative view argues that individuals may display greater skills performing tasks in natural settings, such as at work, where problems are embedded in more familiar, meaningful, and often social contexts. People also have greater internal motivation to develop proficiency in real-life situations. This involves domain-specific knowledge and developing their own heuristics for solving problems that compensate for—or may even be superior to—more formal methods. Such knowledge and techniques are gained through daily experience, learning from others, and participation in a community of practice, and may be tacit rather than easily expressed as formal propositions.

Various case studies in workplace and other settings support this view (Stasz 2001, p. 388). Delivery drivers with near-perfect performance on daily multiplication tasks at work made numerous mistakes on paper-and-pencil test with similar problems (Scribner 1986, p. 19). Brazilian children working as street vendors and subjects asked to troubleshoot a robotics process in an experimental setting exhibited similar discrepancies between real-world and test performance (Stasz 2001, p. 390; Gardner, Chmiel, and Wall 1996); and expert racetrack handicappers perform no better on IQ tests than non-experts (Ceci and Liker 1986, p. 132). Studies of low-scoring military personnel—who were admitted to the armed forces either through a pilot program for disadvantaged applicants or because of mistakes in test-norming—found applicants with usually ineligible scores performed only modestly lower on a wide range of performance measures (Sticht 1992; Stedman and Keastle 1991, p. 118ff.). Other studies of regular enlistees show that performance differences between the lowest- and highest-scoring groups are cut almost in half after a year of job experience, though a permanent gap persists and the lower-scoring groups required longer to reach their maximum potential (Hunt 1995, p. 93). Studies of civilian jobs also consistently find that the correlation between cognitive tests and job performance declines with experience (Hunt 1995, p. 67).

Even analyses using the NALS find that there are large returns to performing reading, writing, and math tasks at work independent of test scores and other covariates, including education (Carbonaro 2002). This implies work-related competencies are partly independent of the skills measured by both educational attainment and cognitive test scores. Interaction models also show that the returns to test scores depend on the frequency with which skills are exercised (Sum 1999; Carbonaro 2002). Thus, the skills workers can develop, and for which they are rewarded, are partly a function of the jobs employers offer, rather than the intrinsic capacities of individuals operating as a hard constraint.[1]

Like Thurow's theory of worker and job queues (1975), this research suggests test scores may rank individuals according to their trainability, but there are real problems in drawing direct conclusions regarding people's absolute capabilities from seemingly analogous tasks on a test. Individuals learn many of the skills needed for their jobs in the context of their jobs and the illustrative tasks used to describe test performance cannot be assumed to describe the practical limits of what people know or can learn. Rewards depend partly on the quality of jobs offered as well as on an individual's own human capital.

This issue of the relationship between test scores and real-world proficiencies can be investigated directly. The NALS system for scoring documents can be used to score reading and math tasks on the job (see for example Fernandez 2001) as well as to score workers' performance on the test, permitting a direct comparison of the two in a validation exercise. The NALS is one of the only methodologies that can compare workers' test scores and the complexity of their job tasks on the same scale. Indeed, methodology used for the NALS is promoted as a tool for investigating workplace literacy demands. Such a validation exercise could provide the first solid evidence on the relationship between test scores and real-world competencies and how they could be equated, but it appears that no such study has been conducted or is planned.

Those associated with the NALS, while not necessarily receptive to the broader critique of testing implied by the situated cognition perspective, recognize some of the complexities discussed above. They caution, "These results do not answer the question, 'Are the literacy skills of our nation's workers adequate?'" (Sum 1999, p. xvi). And they concede that the performance levels "do not enable us to say what specific level of prose, document, or quantitative skill is required to obtain, hold, or advance in a particular occupation" (Kirsch et al. 1993, p. 9). But at other points those responsible for the NALS also contributed to the sense that test results do indeed provide such information:

> For an economy that has supposedly moved into the 'information age' and is becoming dependent on high-performance workplaces to spur economic growth, competitiveness, and productivity, many members of the existing labor force appear ill-equipped with respect to key literacy proficiencies (Sum 1999, p. 33, also see Kirsch et al. 1993, p xxi).

In contrast, a National Center for Education Statistics (NCES) working paper advised those working on a follow-up to the NALS administered in 2002, called the National Assessment of Adult Literacy (NAAL), to learn from the problems associated with the reporting of NALS results:

> All audiences for the NAAL will be longing for simplicity. But the complexities of adult literacy proficiency must be conveyed. Although the public and policymakers will almost certainly be looking to the results of the NAAL to answer the question of how many Americans are 'literate enough,' the designers, reporters, and interpreters of the NAAL should resist the temptation to directly address this question (U.S. Department of Education 2000, p. 26).

International test score comparisons

Although national tests may be better at ranking than at providing mea-sures of absolute competencies, international rankings of test scores explicitly address competitiveness issues while avoiding the problem of inferring absolute competencies, since the concern is specifically to com-pare or rank the cognitive skills of the labor force across nations. Those worried about U.S. skill levels argue that the nation's exceptionally low rankings in international comparisons threaten its economic competi-tiveness. The best data to address this question is the International Adult Literacy Survey (IALS), modeled on the NALS and sponsored and de-veloped by an international team that included Statistics Canada, the Organization for Economic Co-operation and Development (OECD), ETS, and other academics, government agencies, and national study teams. The IALS was administered to representative samples of adults age 16-65 in 21 countries between 1994 and 1998, unfortunately not including Japan.

The IALS results are shown in **Table 4** in ascending order by mean composite score (column 1). The United States is among a lower scor-ing group of advanced industrialized nations that includes most other English-speaking countries, Belgium, and Switzerland, while Germany, the Netherlands, and the Scandinavian countries perform better and the differences are usually significant (p<.05) (OECD and Statistics Canada 2000: 19ff.). Column 2 gives some sense of the scale of the differences by subtracting the U.S. mean from other country means and dividing by the U.S. standard deviation.

The average American is at the 53rd percentile of the pooled sample of all high-income countries participating in the IALS, which is not exceptional but not dire either, despite some portrayals (for example, Sum et al. 2002, p. 30).[2] The United States is not grossly out of step with other countries, although some argue that the scores are not as high as they should be given the higher levels of schooling and per capita education spending in the United States (Sum et al. 2002, p. 19f., 30).

It should be noted that the United States is not the only country dissatisfied with the test results. The French refused to release their test results, arguing that the IALS test was biased in various ways, though French members of the IALS team participated the tests's de-sign and development, and subsequent reviews by an international study

TABLE 4   International Adult Literacy (IALS) test scores, 1994-98

	1 Mean	2 Mean/SD$_{US}$	3 5th pct.	4 95th pct.	5 95/5 ratio	6 (col. 5)/U.S.	7 GDP/U.S.
1. Ireland	263	-0.13	151	353	2.34	0.84	0.72
2. United Kingdom	267	-0.07	145	360	2.48	0.89	0.67
3. Switzerland	271	-0.01	143	352	2.46	0.88	0.84
4. United States	**272**		**133**	**371**	**2.79**		
5. New Zealand	272	0.00	158	361	2.28	0.82	0.55
6. Australia	274	0.03	146	359	2.46	0.88	0.75
7. Belgium	277	0.07	163	359	2.20	0.79	0.74
8. Canada	280	0.12	145	372	2.57	0.92	0.78
9. Germany	285	0.19	208	359	1.73	0.62	0.71
10. Netherlands	286	0.21	202	355	1.76	0.63	0.75
11. Finland	288	0.24	195	363	1.86	0.67	0.68
12. Denmark	289	0.25	213	353	1.66	0.59	0.79
13. Norway	294	0.32	207	363	1.75	0.63	0.85
14. Sweden	304	0.47	216	386	1.79	0.64	0.68

Note: Test scores are from Organization for Economic Cooperation and Development and Statistics Canada (2000: 135f). Test values for Switzerland are averages for three language groups weighted by their share of the population speaking them: German, 70%; French 21%; Italian, 9% (CIA World Factbook). Column 2 divides values from column 1 by the standard deviation for the U.S. sample (sd=68—see Sum et al. 2002: 40). Values in column 6 divide the national ratios of the 95th and 5th percentiles (column 5) by the U.S. ratio. Values in column 7 are per capita GDP for 1998 based on current purchasing power parities divided by the current U.S. GDP, which equaled $32,184 (Statistical Abstract of the United States 2000: 832).

group found no evidence of bias (OECD and Statistics Canada 2000, p. 123ff.).

Moreover, the implications of the IALS results for national economic competitiveness are not obvious. Several high-scoring countries such as the Scandinavian nations and the Netherlands are not usually considered serious economic threats to the United States. Germany's current woes may be attributable to long-standing difficulties in absorbing the former East Germany, which may mask its skills advantage, but this fact in itself suggests the significance of macroeconomic factors, as well as skills, in overall economic performance.

More formally, column 7 of Table 4 shows that U.S. gross domestic product (GDP) per capita (1998) clearly ranks first, despite its test score rank. **Figure 1** shows the relationship between per capita GDP and test scores graphically. Because people in other countries do not work as much as in the United States, **Figure 2** adjusts GDP per capita for differing employment-to-population ratios (International Labor Office 2001, Table 3 [Statistical Annex]), and **Figure 3** makes a further adjustment for differences in hours worked per employee, which the IALS collected on a consistent basis for all countries except Sweden (OECD and Statistics Canada 2000, p. 166). The relationships shown in these graphs are weak, as suggested by the fitted regression lines. Simple correlations between mean test scores and different measures of GDP are -0.02 (Figure 1), -0.27 (Figure 2), and 0.12 (Figure 3) (author's calculations). When Sweden, which is a bit of an outlier, is excluded from the first two calculations to make those samples consistent with the third, the first two correlations rise to 0.12 and -0.11, respectively.

Clearly, the connection between test scores and economic performance is not a very tight one among wealthy industrialized nations, despite the unreflective popular assumption of a close relationship. U.S. economic performance remains comfortably ahead of most other nations by most measures, despite 25 years of concerns over test score trends.

Turning to inequality in test scores, Columns 3 and 4 of Table 4 show the U.S. score at the 5th percentile is quite a bit lower and the score at the 95th percentile rather higher than for most countries. Other researchers calculate that the top quintile in the United States ranks roughly fourth out of 17 nations, while the bottom decile ranks 15th out of 17 (Sum et al. 2002, p. 24). Cognitive skill inequality, measured by

FIGURE 1 Relationship between mean IALS test score and ratio of GDP per capita to U.S.

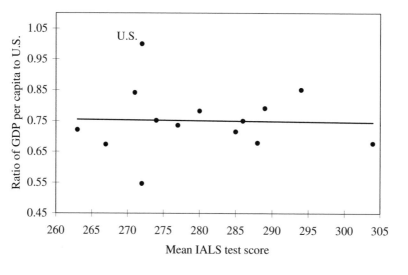

FIGURE 2 Relationship between mean IALS test score and ratio of GDP per capita to U.S. adjusted for employment/population ratio

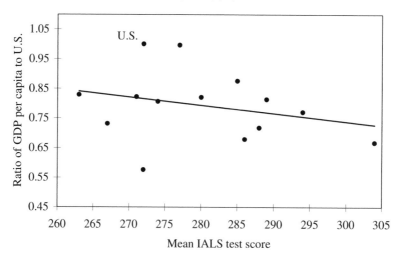

FIGURE 3 Relationship between mean IALS test score and ratio of GDP per capita to U.S. adjusted for annual hours worked

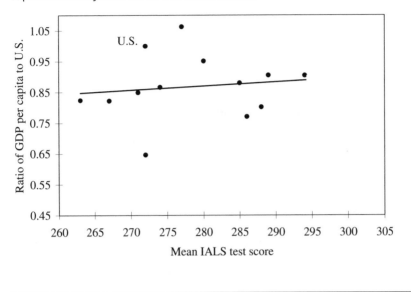

the ratio of scores at the 95th and 5th percentiles, is highest in the United States, especially compared to the group of countries with the highest mean scores (columns 5 and 6) (see also Sum 2002, p. 27).

A later section of this study reviews research on whether workers at the bottom of the U.S. earnings distribution would earn more if they had the skills of their northern European counterparts. Here it is sufficient to note that, when Devroye and Freeman (2001, p. 7) exclude immigrants from samples for the United States, Germany, the Netherlands, and Sweden, they find differences in test score inequality between the United States and the others countries declines by approximately 40%, but earnings inequality within and across countries remains almost unchanged.

Blau and Kahn (2001, p. 23) also find that immigrants account for a considerable portion of the greater test score inequality in the United States relative to eight other countries, when inequality is measured as the difference between scores at the 50th and 10th percentiles. When immigrants are excluded from the samples, the difference between test score inequality in the United States and other countries disappears completely for women and shrinks by 55% for men. "While it might be tempting to conclude that poor quality education is responsible for low U.S. test scores at the bottom, consideration of the native sample suggests that this argument applies only partially to men and perhaps not at all to women" (Blau and Kahn 2001, p. 24; see also Sum et al. 2002, p. 20ff.). The average U.S. immigrant tested in the IALS is at the 17th percentile of the pooled sample (Sum et al. 2002, p. 30).

The OECD also recently administered a standardized reading test to 15-year olds in 27 member countries as part of the Program for International Student Assessment (PISA) (2000). As with the NALS and IALS, ETS was the lead U.S. participant on the international team that developed the test. The U.S. mean score was statistically indistinguishable or greater than the means for all countries except Finland, Canada, and New Zealand, and the standard deviation of U.S. scores is roughly average for the sample of countries. This does not suggest the United States is falling behind other wealthy industrialized nations, at least in reading (OECD 2001).

To further illustrate the difficulties of drawing strong conclusions from individual tests, a comparison of the PISA and IALS country results shows a weak relationship. Published data allow mean scores on the PISA reading test to be compared to mean scores for younger adults (age 26-35) on the prose section of the IALS for most of the countries in Table 4, which is shown in **Figure 4** with a fitted regression line (OECD 2001, p. 84; OECD and Statistics Canada 2000, p. 144).[3] The correlations between the PISA and IALS national means (0.26) and country rankings (0.31) suggest modest convergent validity given that both tested reading ability among similar groups in closely-spaced years and the correlations are based on national-level averages rather than individual-level scores (author's calculations). As with the divergent results for the SAT and ACT within the United States and the moderate correlation between scores on the prose NALS and reading NAEP tests, the IALS-PISA comparison should serve as a caution against drawing overly strong inferences from any single set of test results.

Summary

Although the skills of the workforce have been questioned by many in the skills mismatch camp, reports of declining test scores, educational attainment, and school quality are mostly exaggerated. Scores for young

FIGURE 4 Relationship between national mean PISA score for 15 year-olds (2000) and IALS score for 26-35 year-olds (1994-1998)

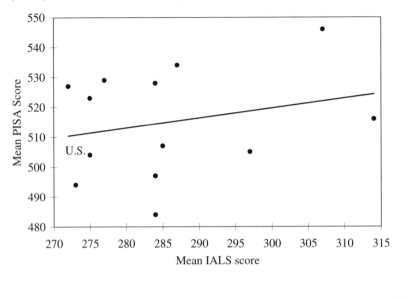

people are as high today as they were 30 years ago, if not higher. And test score inequality has declined, though not uniformly, over this period. NAEP data suggest that stories of absolute cognitive skill declines among young people or recent cohorts have little empirical basis.

Literacy surveys of adults in the 1970s, most of whom completed schooling before the late 1960s, found larger numbers of adults than expected performing poorly even then. NALS (1992) results for adults suggest that more recent cohorts, including those educated since the 1960s, when test scores were declining, have higher literacy than non-elderly older cohorts, even controlling for education.

Of course, if job skill requirements are increasing, then stability or even modest increases in cognitive skills might still imply a growing skills gap in the labor market, especially if skill requirements have increased rapidly.

Attempts to infer real-world capacities from test performance overlook serious obstacles and typically underestimate the complexity of tasks individuals can perform in their daily lives. Perhaps the most telling fact arguing against a literal interpretation of NALS performance levels is that the United States has achieved its current and past levels of economic performance with the people who scored as they did.

International test score comparisons also do not show the United States performing particularly poorly relative to other advanced industrialized countries; nor does its test-score rank reflect its relative economic performance.

CHAPTER 3

Job skill requirements: trends and cross-sectional evidence

Background

> What percentage of U.S. workers need to know how to prepare a budget? Or need to know principles of electricity? What percentage of U.S. workers need to be able to do arithmetic computation to perform their jobs effectively? Or need good eye-hand coordination? Or need to be able to make effective oral presentations to groups? The answer to all these questions is unknown. (Pearlman 1997, p. 155)

If, as suggested by the last chapter, it is difficult to determine precisely the skills workers have, it is even more difficult to know the skills employers require them to use at work. Although many observers believe it is a truism that work in the information age is becoming more skilled and that the pace of skill upgrading is accelerating, there is limited hard data on the subject. Ultimately, there are simply few detailed sources of information on what people actually do at work. Research strategies have included analysis of trends in the distribution of workers across occupations, mean education by occupation, and the well-known direct measures of job complexity from the *Dictionary of Occupational Titles* (DOT), but all have well-known limitations (Spenner 1990). Proprietary job analysis techniques used by human resource consulting firms do exist, but such data are generally not available to researchers and the representativeness of their norming samples is unknown. Qualitative case studies have used unstandardized approaches and produced divergent findings whose general applicability is also unknown.

The quality of the DOT data has provoked particular concern (Cain and Treiman 1981; Spenner 1990; Attewell 1990), not all of it necessarily justified (Handel 2000). However, one indication of the scarcity of this kind of information is the fact that even much current research on skill has been forced to rely on DOT measures (for example, Eliason 1995; Tam 1997; Devereaux 2000), most of which were collected in the 1960s with significant updating in the 1970s (Cain and Treiman 1981) and more modest revisions again in the 1980s.

For a topic that has provoked so much interest, there has been surprisingly little effort to develop a standard methodology or scheme for rating job skill demands and to apply it across time for large, representative samples. The Department of Labor is developing a replacement for the DOT, called the Occupational Information Network (O*NET), but whether it will be useful for researchers is uncertain (National Research Council 1999, p. 201ff., 321ff.).

Also complicating efforts to understand job skill requirements are variations in skill requirements within occupations across employers and even within employers over time, depending on cyclical variations or secular changes in the quality of the available labor (Bills 1992a; Holzer, Raphael, and Stoll 2003, p. 27f.). This shifting landscape means that in many cases skill requirements are more a range than a single point. Even staunch advocates of IQ as the best predictor of appropriate job qualifications acknowledge test scores vary widely among people in the same occupation and the test score distributions of most occupations overlap one another (Gottfredson 1997, p. 87ff.).

One matched employer-employee sample found that as many as 26% of recently hired high school dropouts had jobs that their employers reported "required" a high school diploma, though such educationally "underqualified" employees accounted for a relatively small share of the total sample (Moss and Tilly 2001, p. 54, 82).

Research on workers with less education than their jobs "require" finds that their pay is lower than employees in the same kind of jobs who have the specified education, but higher than those with the same education who hold jobs matched to their (lower) education level (Duncan and Hoffman 1981; Sicherman 1991; Cohn and Khan 1995). It is possible that the "underqualified" are at the upper end of the cognitive skill distribution within their education group; most studies do not control for test scores.

However, it is also possible that general job requirements are not as constraining as imagined because occupation-specific skills or other job requirements, such as interpersonal skills or motivation and work habits, are more important or because the skills needed in that context can be acquired through work experience.

Indeed, despite claims that wage inequality growth in the 1980s reflected declining demand for less skilled workers, the wage penalty for undereducation did not increase during that time (Daly et al. 2000). Likewise, while the incidence of undereducation rose, the size of the change did not differ from similar changes in the early 1970s, when wage inequality was stable (Handel 2000).

Despite these difficulties for the skills mismatch thesis, there is no lack of observers and researchers willing to assert that skill demands are increasing substantially, whether due to the spread of computers, employee involvement programs, or—in the case of interpersonal skills—the growing share of service sector jobs. A recent report on the NAEP writing assessment affirms that most students have basic writing skills, but then proceeds to claim, without any supporting evidence, that employer demands are rising: "The difficulty is that [students] cannot systematically produce [write] at the high levels of skill, maturity, and sophistication required in a complex, modern economy" (National Commission on Writing in America's Schools and Colleges 2003, p. 16). This conclusion was duly reported in the mass media (in the April 26 *Chicago Tribune*, for example). Even econometric studies that find the skills gap owes more to a slowdown in the growth of supply than changes in demand spend much of their time trying to show a relationship between the spread of workplace computer use and the growth of demand for skill (Autor et al. 1998).

This chapter reviews general research on changing job skill requirements. Studies of the specific effects of rising computer use and employee involvement practices are reviewed elsewhere (Handel 2003; Handel and Levine 2004). In general, trend studies indicate a shift toward jobs requiring more skills, but there is little evidence that the rate of change accelerated in the last two decades, as would be the case if trends in employers' requirements were responsible for the growth in wage inequality. Cross-sectional studies often suggest employers are less concerned about cognitive skills deficits than what they consider poor work habits, motivation, demeanor, and attitudes.

Trend analyses

Occupational studies

Spenner's (1979) well-known work using DOT job ratings found little net change in mean job skill requirements or modest upgrading over time. Despite questions over methodology (Cain and Treiman 1981), Spenner reviewed a number of other studies that reinforced his original conclusion pointing to moderate and gradual skill upgrading over time (Spenner 1988).

By contrast, the Hudson Institute's *Workforce 2000* report (Johnston and Packer 1987), also using the DOT, argued strongly that the demand for skills was rising rapidly and inducing a gap between skills workers possesed and the those required by their jobs. The report's bold claims garnered both widespread attention and subsequent criticism, though the criticism received much less attention.

The report claimed that by 2000, "even the least-skilled jobs will require a command of reading, computing, and thinking that was once necessary only for the professions," and every high school graduate will need the ability to "solve complex problems requiring algebra and statistics" (Johnston and Packer 1987, p. 116), although the Bureau of Labor Statistics (BLS) occupational projections and DOT ratings used in the report's analyses did not support such sweeping conclusions. "Unless the nation is able to bring even its least able workers up to higher standards of education and skills, it is likely that average rates of unemployment will rise," especially for disadvantaged minorities, who were forecast to increase rapidly as a proportion of the labor force (Johnston and Packer 1987, p. 96ff.).

It is hard to see how the authors could have been very optimistic about achieving such advanced capabilities in such a short time when they also cite NAEP results to make the familiar claim that large numbers of young adults "lack even the basic skills essential for employment....only a quarter of whites, 7% of Hispanics, and 3% of blacks could decipher a bus schedule; only 44% of whites, 20% of Hispanics, and 8% of blacks could correctly determine the change they were due from the purchase of a two-item restaurant meal" (Johnston and Packer 1987, p. 102f.).

As Chapter 2 indicated, these kinds of extrapolations from test scores to real-world competencies cannot be taken at face value. Even *Workforce*

2000 hedges when it concludes that DOT measures indicate *middle-skill* jobs require only that workers "read and understand directions, add and subtract, and be able to speak and think clearly" (Johnston and Packer 1987, p. 100). The authors predict these jobs will comprise the lower part of the job distribution in the future, but this more restrained judgment contradicts the report's more prominent claims.

In addition, the forecasts in *Workforce 2000* were compromised by what most recognize today as methodological sleights of hand. The report never presented a simple breakdown of the current and projected distribution of skill requirements, and it did not report estimates of the rate of skill upgrading overall. Instead, it reported trends mostly in terms of the skill demands of selected occupations predicted to grow or decline rapidly in percentage terms, even though occupations growing at a fast rate often account for a small number of jobs in absolute terms. The report also calculated the skill levels of "net new jobs," defined as jobs that exceeded replacement levels within different occupations, an approach that did not account for other sources of future job vacancies, such as turnover and retirement in existing positions. Because both rapidly growing occupations and "net new jobs" tend to account for small proportions of all jobs, the report exaggerated the pace of change.

A California report modeled on *Workforce 2000* and using the same methodology was more straightforward, predicting that the percentage of jobs in that state requiring only 8th grade math would drop from 78.1% to 76.9% between 1987 and 2000 and those requiring only 8th grade verbal skills would drop from 58.3% to 56.5%, indicating an upgrading in skill requirements but not exactly a seismic shift (California Workforce Literacy Task Force 1991).

With the passage of time, readily available Census occupational breakdowns can give a first rough test of the idea that the skill upgrading process has accelerated. **Table 5** shows a consistent trend toward skill upgrading, at least as a function of shifts between major occupations, contradicting earlier "de-skilling" predictions. However, the growth rate of the high-skill managerial and professional categories and the shrinkage of traditional blue-collar occupations have both decelerated over time, especially between 1990 and 2000, contrary to predictions of acceleration. In addition, despite the dire forecasts of *Workforce 2000* that many Americans would be unprepared for the new economy, neither the unemployment rate nor the employment-to-population ratio

TABLE 5 Trends in the distribution of workers across major occupations, 1970-2000

	Year				Growth rate		
	1970	1980	1990	2000	1970-80	1980-90	1990-2000
Manager	7.5	10.4	12.3	14.6	2.9	1.9	2.3
Professional	11.1	12.3	14.1	15.6	1.2	1.8	1.5
Technical	2.3	3.1	3.7	3.2	0.8	0.6	-0.5
Total	*20.9*	*25.8*	*30.1*	*33.4*	*4.9*	*4.3*	*3.3*
Sales	10.2	10.0	11.8	12.1	-0.2	1.8	0.3
Clerical	16.5	17.3	16.3	13.8	0.8	-1.0	-2.5
Service	12.7	12.9	13.2	13.5	0.2	0.3	0.3
Farming	3.8	2.9	2.5	2.5	-0.9	-0.4	0.0
Crafts	14.1	12.9	11.3	11.0	-1.2	-1.6	-0.3
Oper./labor	21.8	18.3	14.8	13.5	-3.5	-3.5	-1.3
Total	*35.9*	*31.2*	*26.1*	*24.5*	*-4.7*	*-5.1*	*-1.6*
Unemployment	4.9	7.1	5.6	4.0	2.2	-1.5	-1.6
Empl./population	57.4	59.2	62.8	64.5	1.8	3.6	1.7
Males	76.2	72.0	72.0	71.8	-4.2	0.0	-0.2
Females	40.8	47.7	54.3	57.7	6.9	6.6	3.4

Sources: U.S. Bureau of the Census 1989, Statistical Abstract of the United States 2001, Economic Report of the President.

show obvious deterioration, though analysis by education level would be necessary to see if the overall picture masks compositional changes that might be more consistent with skill mismatch predictions.

Other, more formal studies using BLS occupational data and DOT ratings reach similar conclusions. They show the growth in skill requirements did not accelerate in the 1980s and 1990s relative to the 1960s and 1970s, nor did BLS projections for the 1990s imply such acceleration (Howell and Wolff 1991; Mishel and Teixeira 1991, p. 28ff.; Handel 2000; for Britain, see Robinson 1998).

Howell and Wolff (1991) find that growing skill demands did not translate into wage growth because service industries and female-dominated occupations accounted for much of the job growth. Service industries have higher average skills but lower average wages than manufacturing and other male-dominated jobs. This disconnect between wage and skill trends supports the segmented labor markets notion that certain jobs are relatively well-paid because of institutional conditions rather than human capital requirements and suggests that wage inequality growth partly reflects the declining number of such jobs relative to those in secondary labor markets.

Sum (1999, p. 94) and Barton (2000, p. 15, 19) examine trends in skill requirements by assigning mean NALS scores to occupations instead of DOT job ratings. They use BLS data and projections of trends in the occupational composition of employment and find that occupational shifts leave literacy requirements almost completely unchanged for the 1990-2005 and 1986-2006 periods, respectively. "Unless substantive upgrading of literacy-related skills occurs within occupations, these data provide little evidence of a major skills mismatch due to higher literacy requirements in future jobs" (Sum 1999, p. 95). Of course, if one believes that a more skilled job structure than projected is socially desirable, even stability may be cause for concern.

These studies effectively refute the conclusions of *Workforce 2000* (Johnston and Packer 1987). The Hudson Institute recently issued an updated report, *Workforce 2020* (1997), that reaffirms the conclusions of the previous report but it was not consulted for this review.

Also consistent with findings of limited change, studies using the General Social Survey (GSS) vocabulary test do not find any consistent tendency for an increasing association between test scores and occupation across cohorts or between test scores and either occupational status or earnings between the early 1970s and mid-1990s for all cohorts (Weakliem et al. 1995; Hauser and Huang 1997).

Cappelli (1993) is one of the few studies that has data on skill shifts within occupations as well as skill shifts resulting from changes in the occupational distribution. The study uses two waves of proprietary job ratings from the compensation consulting firm Hay Associates. Unfortunately, the data are limited to production and clerical workers in the late 1970s to the mid-1980s. Cappelli finds that the "Hay points" (or job ratings) of production workers rose 8% between 1978 and 1986, roughly two-thirds of this rise due to the increased scores of detailed production occupations and remaining third due to changes in the distribution of workers across those occupations. Upgrading among clerical occupations was more modest, and within-occupation and between-occupation shifts each accounted for half of the overall ratings growth. However, it is hard to know how to evaluate the magnitude of these changes, nor can they be compared to prior or subsequent rates of change, and even the representativeness of the samples is unclear.

Employer surveys

The cross-sectional National Employers Survey (NES) (1994) asked employers for retrospective information on trends in job skill demands. The survey found 57% of employers reported skill requirements and training for production or other front-line jobs had increased in the previous three years and almost all of the rest reported stability rather than declines for both items. However, there is no way to assess whether the magnitude of the upgrading was great or slight in either an absolute sense or relative to past trends, whether the retrospective assessments are reliable, or how these establishment-level figures translate into incidence rates for the workforce (National Center on the Educational Quality of the Workforce 1994).

The Rural Manufacturing Survey (RMS) (1996) asked questions similar to the NES. The survey was conducted by the Economic Research Service of the Department of Agriculture and, despite its title, includes a large urban subsample. The RMS found that roughly 15% of employers reported basic reading and math skill requirements rose "a lot" in the previous three years, 50-60% reported no change, and 32-40% reported computer and interpersonal/teamwork skills requirements rose "a lot." Although most relevant to the next chapter on mismatch, it is worth pointing out that, even with this reported upgrading, only 5-15% of employers reported "major" problems in finding qualified applicants for production jobs requiring any of these skills. The largest problem was finding workers with a "reliable and acceptable work attitude," cited by approximately 30% of employers (Teixeira 1998).

The Multi-City Study of Urban Inequality (MCSUI) (1992-94) also asked employers in four cities (Atlanta, Boston, Detroit, and Los Angeles) retrospective questions about skill changes in jobs requiring no more than a high school degree. Some 40% reported skill requirements rose in the previous five to 10 years, and only about 1% reported declining skill requirements (Moss and Tilly 2001, p. 54ff.). Responses were evenly split on whether the new skill demands were cognitive (basic reading, writing, and math) or social and communication skills. The most commonly cited reasons for the trends were new technology, especially computers, and organizational changes, followed by changes in product quality and services and greater customer contact, though some of the specific rankings varied by occupation (clerical, customer service, blue collar).

However, there is no way to determine the magnitude of the change in skill requirements from this data. Employers who reported increased skill demands in the MCSUI survey were as likely to have decreased as increased their level of screening for job applicants. Qualitative interviews also suggested generally modest changes in hiring and screening methods. Many employers indicated that most new computer skills were fairly basic and easily learned. Though some employers reported that record-keeping and other basic literacy requirements of jobs had increased, more emphasized the increased need for social skills and motivation, the latter often linked to a more competitive business environment and leaner staffing patterns (Moss and Tilly 2001, p. 63ff.).

Other studies of trends in job skill requirements
In one of the most thorough and rigorous studies of skill change, Fernandez (2001) conducted extensive observations and interviews and administered two waves of surveys in a single factory before and after its relocation from an antiquated facility to a new, state-of-the-art automated plant. Management also adopted a new employee involvement philosophy giving workers greater discretion and more decision-making, problem-solving, and record-keeping functions. Using an impressive variety of measures, Fernandez shows convincingly that skill demands rose after the changeover.

However, there are reasons to question whether the increase was qualitatively large. Workers' self-reports regarding the use of reading, writing, and math in the new plant were only modestly higher than before (0.32 on a 5-point scale). The average number of documents workers used on the job rose from 2.6 to 10.3, not counting a large number of computer screen forms, but the documents' qualitative complexity, which was rated using the system employed on the National Adult Literacy Survey, seems to have increased only modestly. The absolute reading and math demands remain fairly simple. A typical change: new requirements to use decimals and read graphs, compared to only basic arithmetic needed in the old plant.

Workers in the first wave of surveys reported their jobs required 10 years of formal education, while the second wave, administered after the plant changeover, yielded a figure of 11.5 years. But even the higher figure is roughly equal to the average level of education of workers in the original plant, so there does not appear to be a gap between the skills required by the new system and those workers already possessed. The average training time also remained constant. Fernandez seems to acknowledge at various points that the existing workforce could absorb the skill upgrading relatively easily.

Indeed, one of the most telling pieces of evidence against a skills mismatch reading of the Fernandez study is the plant management's no-layoff pledge to its workers, which meant that the vast majority of those working at the new site had been employed at the previous plant. Measures of turnover were unaffected by the move and the plant's racial composition remained unchanged (55% minority), despite widespread fears of a mismatch between the skills of minorities and those demanded by high-tech work environments.

Despite "massive upgrading" (Fernandez 2001, 279) of the production technology, only one job was totally automated away and the plant had no difficulty maintaining total employment at previous levels (roughly 200 hourly workers). The new equipment did lead to the hiring of three additional maintenance electricians and six additional maintenance mechanics because of the increased cost of machine downtime.

The additional craft jobs and pay raises that brought their jobs closer to parity with prevailing wages in the regional labor market increased wage inequality among production workers. Because the company guaranteed no cuts in nominal wages for production workers, Fernandez concludes that actual wage inequality would have grown more had the company hired a new workforce for the new plant or allowed operatives' pay to fall to its market rate, as well.

However, in some respects this case overstates what can be extrapolated to the economy overall. The complete substitution of a technologically backward plant with a state-of-the-art facility is a more dramatic change than is typical of technological change within individual plants, so the magnitude of the skill shifts recorded by Fernandez are likely an extreme-case estimate of what one might expect from automation and employee involvement within a plant or the economy overall for the short- and medium-run. The skill shifts in this and similar plants would have to be averaged over the experience of more typical plants that experience less or no technological change in a given year to estimate the annual change in aggregate skill demand. The already rather modest skill changes in plants like this one experiencing dramatic changes in production technology will be diluted considerably when the experience of more typical establishments is taken into account.

There is also no way to know if the change Fernandez documents represents an acceleration relative to past trends. For example, it has long been noted that more automated plants employ relatively more skilled maintenance workers (Woodward 1965). This kind of occupational shift is easily tracked for the overall economy through standard labor force statistics, and they do not indicate that craft workers have grown as a percentage of all workers (Handel 2000).

More scattered trend data is also available from labor force surveys with items on job requirements and training.

In the Panel Study of Income Dynamics, the percentage of respondents saying they needed work experience or a special skill, in addition to required education, in order to obtain their current job increased from 60.5% (1976) to 71.1% (1985), but the absence of a longer time series makes it impossible to know whether this represents acceleration relative to past trends (Handel 2000, p. 254).

Training supplements to the Current Population Survey (CPS) for January 1983 and January 1991 indicate little change in workers' needs for specific skills or training to obtain their current job (55% versus 57%), and the figures actually *declined* for workers under age 35, contradicting expectations that young workers were especially likely to face greater skill demands in restructured jobs. The number receiving training after obtaining their current job rose from 35% to 41% between 1983 and 1991, mostly due to increased formal training provided by employers, but, again, the percentage barely changed for younger workers, and data from the Quality of Employment Surveys show much faster growth in the 1970s (Handel 2000, p. 254). Analyses of the CPS supplements indicate that the growth in training accounts for little of the growth in the returns to education in the 1980s (Constantine and Neumark 1996).

The 1993 wave of the National Longitudinal Survey of Youth (NLSY) (1979) indicates that 40% of workers age 28-36 experienced workplace changes that required them to learn new job skills in the previous year consistent with skill upgrading (Leigh and Gifford 1999). However, the median length of the new training seems to total only two days or so for all workers, though the mean may be closer to seven days for those receiving training (author's calculation from Leigh and Gifford, Table 3).

The NLSY also asked the reasons for receiving training: 15-20% cited the introduction of new equipment, new products, need to upgrade computer skills, and the creation of work teams, but only 2% of these young workers, who were among the lower-scoring cohorts on the NAEP (1974-82), reported their employer needed to upgrade workers' basic reading, writing, and math skills (author's calculation from Leigh and Gifford, Table 2).[4] This finding is consistent with results for the overall workforce from the January 1991 CPS, which found that only 3-5% of blue-collar and lower white-collar workers ever received basic skills training from their current employers (U.S. Department of Labor 1992).

While the introduction of work teams and other organizational reforms were significant predictors of basic skills upgrading, as much of the literature on high-performance work systems predicts, their effects were modest (Leigh and Gifford 1999, p. 189).

For all the hand-wringing over workers' basic skills, especially the cohort surveyed by the NLSY, few firms apparently felt much impulse to improve them. It appears that most employees are able to absorb technological and organizational changes with just a few days of training, which typically does not include basic skills training.

It is possible that employers who are most likely to change their technology and organization are also more selective in recruiting employees, so they have less need to upgrade their workers' basic skills. Nevertheless, given that 40% of the workers in the NLSY participated in some training in the prior year, it is remarkable that only 2% of workers received basic skills training.

Traditional human capital models argue that firms will not engage in general training for fear of poaching, but in the absence of certification it is unclear that workers receiving remedial basic skills instruction are prime candidates for poaching, nor is it obvious that other, more prevalent kinds of training—such as teamwork or computer training—do not have a general training aspect as well. Perhaps employer behavior is explained by social role conceptions that make them resistant to taking on an educational remediation role. However, it seems equally likely that employers do not provide much basic skills training because they do not consider it necessary. This possibility is reinforced by the brevity of training for new technology, new product introductions, computer skill upgrading, and introduction of work teams. Employers seem to judge it sufficient to provide their current workforce with short periods of training to adjust to these changes, though the possibility that this level of training is less than optimal cannot be excluded.

Cross-sectional studies

Cross-sectional information on employer skill demands comes from survey and case study research, which often have richer measures than time series based on the DOT or retrospective employer reports. This section also draws on various policy- or practitioner-oriented compilations of results from employer focus groups and interviews, whose quality is much more mixed.

Employer surveys
Employer data from the MCSUI project found that more than half of jobs requiring less than a college education require daily reading of paragraphs, arithmetic, computer use, and dealing with customers, and 30% of such jobs require daily writing of paragraphs. Between two-thirds and three-quarters of these jobs required a high school degree, general work experience, and job-specific work experience, but roughly 80% were also open to hiring applicants with GED degrees and welfare recipients (Holzer 1996, p. 49ff.).

Although the CPS is not an employer survey, the January 1991 supplement asked a national sample of workers similar questions about their job duties. Roughly 30% of workers with no more than a high school degree reported daily reading, writing, and computer use, significantly lower than Holzer's estimates, but the figure is closer for arithmetic or math (55%). Corresponding percentages for workers with more than a high school degree were approximately 20 points higher (Handel 2000). Unfortunately, neither the CPS nor the MCSUI survey has information on the complexity of the reading, writing, math, and other tasks workers perform on their jobs.

Crain (1984) addresses this issue in the only nationally representative survey of hiring managers found for this review. The sampling frame was employer contact information given by respondents to the National Longitudinal Study (NLS-1972) in the 1976 and 1979 waves, when the respondents were 22 and 25 years old, respectively. The survey was conducted in 1983 and sent to the respondents' workplaces. Questions referred to the respondents' occupations but did not allude to the respondent. One item gave a list of 16 employee characteristics for employers to rate. Some 65% of employers said it was extremely important that employees be "able to read materials about as difficult as the daily newspaper" and 57% said the same for the ability "to accurately add, subtract, multiply, and divide," but only 22% said the same for "being able to read complex materials," and only 11% for being able to "handle complex calculations" (Crain 1984, p. 24). More frequently mentioned as important were dependability (94%) and proper attitude (82%), as well as more generic skills such as "good judgment" (62%) and "quick learner" (57%), mentioned in similar proportions as basic reading and math (Crain 1984, p. 40). In other words, this survey found employers mostly want high school graduates to have basic cognitive skills, desirable work habits, and common sense.

Other data also suggest that the importance of cognitive skills can be exaggerated relative to interpersonal skills and work habits. Employers in the MCSUI survey were as likely to consider an applicant's politeness and motivation important as they were to value the applicant's English or verbal skills; employers also considered physical appearance and neatness important. Half of the employers were reluctant to hire those with spotty work histories, and two-thirds would not accept someone with a criminal record. Holzer concludes that employers place as much emphasis on factors that are "signals of general employability and readiness for work, rather than...measures of specific skills" (Holzer 1996, p. 60).

The NES found that on a 5-point scale, employers' top two criteria in hiring non-supervisory and production workers were applicants' attitudes (4.6) and communication skills (4.2), followed by previous work experience (4.0). Years of schooling (2.9), grades (2.5), and even scores on pre-employment tests and industry-based credentials (3.2) were considerably further down the list (National Center on the Educational Quality of the Workforce 1994). Focus groups of employers often lapsed into embarrassed silence when asked what specific skills they wanted schools to teach their future employees, followed by comments that emphasized the need for reliability, trainability, and self-motivation. Many employers said they refused to hire applicants under age 26 (Zemsky 1997, p. 53; Applebome 1995). Numerous other surveys of employers conducted by polling groups or human resource consultants also indicate that employers place greatest importance on attitudes and work habits in hiring, and they find these to be the characteristics in shortest supply (Cappelli 1995; O'Neil et al. 1992; Bills 1992b, p. 14f.; Crain 1984, p. 34).

A director of the NES study commented on the results of employer focus groups:

> We were surprised at just how much animosity there is toward young people in the employer community….In the focus groups the response was almost scatological. It's not clear how much this really had to do with young people and how much it's just something in the culture now that young people get dumped upon. (Applebome 1995)

A case study of a business association involved in education reform also found employers complained more about young workers' lack of discipline and motivation than their poor cognitive skills. It should be pointed out, however, that the low wages, slim promotion opportunities, and relative insecurity of the jobs available to young people—and even increasingly to adults with only a high school education—might be responsible for some of the low motivation employers complain about (Ray and Mickelson 1993).

Rosenbaum and Binder (1997) found employers put more emphasis on cognitive skills of potential employees. Their qualitative interviews with more than 50 Chicago-area employers in various industries that offer entry-level jobs suitable for high school graduates found that roughly 70% required basic academic skills.

However, a study of similar jobs finds far fewer skill demands, at least at the entry level. Where reading was required, it was episodic and the texts were short and declarative, required little interpretation and analysis, and rarely exceeded 8th or 9th grade levels. Writing or math requirements were even less common. Most math tasks were simple computations, except for some more complicated multi-step operations performed by those working on mutual fund accounts or in an accounting department (Hughes et al. 1999).

Bowles and Gintis (2002) cite the NES findings and other, similar results as evidence for their long-held view that workers are rewarded for their willingness to follow managers' directions and other workplace norms as much as for the cognitive skills emphasized by human capital theory. Their review of numerous studies finds that the inclusion of cognitive test scores in standard wage equations reduces the education coefficient by only about 18% on average, leaving 82% of education's effect on wages unexplained by cognitive skills and presumably reflecting the effect of schooling in socializing people in ways employers value. Both cognitive skills and years of education are strongly associated with earnings, but they appear to be largely independent of one another and the inclusion of test scores in a standard human capital model increases R^2 by only 0.01, on average. The main value of education in this view is that it signals to employers that workers are more or less reliable, responsible, hard-working, self-disciplined, liable to take more initiative, and relatively confident of their ability to produce desired results.

Though previous attempts to test directly for the effects of personality measures on wages often produced weak results, a recent study using the Panel Study of Income Dynamics finds effects rivaling those of education itself, and accounting for 37% of education's effect on wages before conditioning on the personality measures (Duniform and Duncan 1998; Bowles and Gintis 2002, p. 11). Similar research using the NLSY finds weaker but significant effects of self-esteem on wages (Murnane et al. 2001). Meta-analyses from industrial psychology show strong effects of personality variables, often labeled "conscientiousness," on earnings and low correlations between personality and cognitive test scores (Bowles and Gintis 2002). Research indicates that dependability and other pro-social organizational behaviors receive equal weight in supervisory ratings as technical performance and are best predicted by personality measures (Borman et al. 1997).

Case studies

Case studies provide more detail on skills used on the job but further illustrate the difficulty of determining the relative importance of cognitive skill demands.

Based on a study of two auto plants, Murnane and Levy (1996, p. 23ff.) argue that high levels of employee involvement demand high levels of skill. A joint venture between Mitsubishi and Chrysler used a standard cognitive skills test, the General Assessment Test Battery, and set cutoff scores at the 50-70 percentiles of national norms, depending on the sub-test, which is a relatively high threshold for assembly work. Screening also included team, quality improvement, and sample work exercises, in addition to videos on the corporate culture and interviews with managers, supervisors, and existing workers. A validation study indicated that, among those hired, there was no correlation between test scores and supervisor ratings, but performance in the team exercises and interviews, which were not highly correlated with test scores, did predict supervisor evaluations.

By contrast, another auto plant Murnane and Levy studied, operated by Honda, used a lower selection standard. The plant used a test of middle school math, such as interpreting line and bar graphs and converting fractions into percentages, and a reading test that requires careful understanding but no interpretation of text passages, which most applicants pass.

Levin (1994, p. 99) reports that a Toyota plant in Kentucky spent nearly 90% of its hiring process selecting for work commitment and teamwork skills. Toyota's successful NUMMI plant, run jointly with General Motors in northern California, also restructured and achieved dramatic productivity gains with mostly former GM workers screened using a 20-minute basic math test.

Graham (1993, p. 157f.) also found that corporate culture and inculcation of appropriate work attitudes accounted for 55% of the three-week, full-time orientation and training period in an Isuzu transplant in Indiana. Practical matters—such as work rules, human resource policies, and hard skills training in reading blueprints, quality control, and conducting time studies—accounted for the rest. Still, this plant required applicants to score in the 85th percentile on a four-hour aptitude test—even higher than the plants studied by Murnane and Levy—which may have reduced the time necessary for hard skills training. However, understanding the rationale for different test cutoffs in different plants requires more information about the size of the available labor supply in each location, as well as the intrinsic cognitive demands of the jobs themselves.

Levin (1998b) wondered why Mercedes and BMW recently chose to locate their U.S. plants in rural South Carolina and Alabama—states with among the lowest test scores and levels of educational investment—if skills are an increasingly important consideration. A potent consideration is surely that these states are located far from the high-wage, unionized industrial heartland and that their state governments pursue aggressively pro-business policies, such as subsidies, low taxes, "right-to-work" laws, and other measures tending to make for low wages. Levin suggests that threshold literacy skills are necessary for these jobs but that physical productivity depends more on management practices and levels of capital investment.

Smith's (1999) detailed study of the math used by production workers in 16 auto plants finds generally very modest math requirements, ubiquitous use of calculators, and only modestly higher demands at Japanese transplants. Typical tasks involved measurement, counting, arithmetic with whole numbers, and reading, interpreting, and recording numerical information. Digital measuring devices and more automated production equipment tended to simplify math tasks compared to older, manual tools and equipment. Decimal computations were usually performed with calculators. Often, workers only needed to follow procedures in rote fashion without understanding the meaning of numbers they used or the calculations they performed.

Three plants, including two Japanese transplants, required more frequent and complex math tasks, such as more operations with decimals, calculation of ratios, and conversion among fractions, decimals, and percentages. Team leaders sometimes used algebraic formulae, but everyone had access to calculators for all computations.

Only machinists and highly skilled quality workers at one plant required higher math (such as trigonometry) or worked with computerized equipment that required complex geometric and spatial skills. Aside from these cases, Smith concluded, "The equivalent of an eighth-grade mathematics education is adequate preparation for modern, nonprofessional work," though he acknowledged that to some extent job tasks are specifically designed around the perceived limitations of workers and some workers may initially have had difficulties even with these tasks (Smith 1999, p. 871).

The generally modest level of skill requirements is also consistent with a literacy audit performed at a Motorola plant that embarked on one of the most thorough employee involvement programs in a company known as a leader in this area (Gogan 1994). Occupational analysts concluded that 8th grade math skills (four functions, decimals, fractions, mixed numbers) and 9th grade reading skills were reasonable expectations even for jobs transformed by the introduction of high-performance work practices; most writing required only filling out forms or transferring information from one source to another (Henning et al. 1992).

These are the kinds of skills that would seem relatively simple to teach in short classes using sample work documents (known as a functional context approach and drawing on the situated cognition perspective in psychology), though adult education may involve some anxiety and role strain for students and work disruption for employers.

Outside blue-collar work, Murnane and Levy (1996) found that an insurance company increased job skill requirements after adopting a stronger customer service orientation and more integrated computer databases to cope with increased product market competition. The company broadened job tasks and required more integrated knowledge of customer accounts. The proportion of customer service representatives who were four-year college grads rose from 8% (1981) to 20% (1991) because managers valued both their specific cognitive skills and ability to learn new things and their greater communication skills and reliability.

Bailey and Bernhardt (1997) generally found little or no meaningful change in job duties or skill requirements in retail businesses that claimed to be implementing employee involvement practices.

Policy-oriented reports

Aside from academic research, there is a policy- and practitioner-oriented literature. Some of these works are sensible and reasoned inventories and evaluations of employers' expressed needs (Hollenbeck 1994). Others, such as the well-known report from Labor Secretary's Commission on Achieving Necessary Skills (SCANS) (U.S. Department of Labor 1991) produced little more than rather obvious and general guidelines, such as the need for all workers to have effective reading, writing, math, problem-solving, and interpersonal skills, and desirable personal characteristics such as high motivation and integrity, but nothing more specific. A similar, more detailed inventory included items such as the need to "use the tools and equipment necessary to get the job done." Not surprisingly, when it was "validated" in a survey of 2,500 Michigan employers, "all the skills were rated as very important" (O'Neil et al. 1992, p. 8). These kinds of "hortatory guidelines" (Levin 1998b), undifferentiated by level of complexity or the kind or number of jobs to which they apply, add little to our knowledge of actual skill demands, although they seem popular with various blue-ribbon commissions and business groups.

Summary

Trend data indicate that job skill requirements are rising, but not more rapidly than in the past. Even given this growth, few studies report that cognitive skill requirements are high in an absolute sense for jobs filled by high-school-educated workers, though the data is not strong in this area and the modest demand for higher skills in these jobs may partly reflect employer adjustments to the limits of their workforce.

Many studies also suggest that employers place as much or greater weight on non-cognitive factors, such as work effort and cooperative attitudes. The upgrading effects of technology and employee involvement on skill requirements also appear modest (see also Handel 2003; Handel and Levine 2004). However, there is also clearly a need for improved data on trends in job skill requirements and their causes.

The question of whether even the gradual changes detected have strained the abilities of the available workforce remains unanswered and available evidence on this subject is reviewed in the next chapter.

CHAPTER 4

Evidence for skills mismatch

Background

Reviewing research on workers' skills and employers' requirements separately—and separate from the question of any mismatch between them—reflects the fact that the different studies examining these issues use incommensurate measures of skills. Consequently, the evidence on the question of mismatch is even more indirect and fragmentary than what is available for discussion of either side of this equation taken individually. This situation indicates the need for a better framework for subsequent data collection that will permit researchers to compare the skills of workers and the requirements of jobs using a common yardstick.

Additional considerations and problems arise in trying to examine the notion of a skills mismatch.

The concept of skills mismatch or skills shortage requires clarification. One can define skills mismatch or skills shortage as a situation in which some workers want employment or more work hours and employers have unmet labor needs but will not draw from the underemployed group at existing wages because those workers' skills are inadequate.

In neoclassical economics, fully flexible wages equilibrate supply and demand efficiently, so any imbalance should be temporary. Skilled workers' wages are bid up until enough employers no longer want to hire more workers of this type and the number of positions equals the number of job-seekers. Likewise, less-skilled workers' wages fall until the surplus labor force disappears, either because the unemployed are reabsorbed into employment or because workers facing unacceptably low wages exit the labor market. Thus, mismatches or shortages are temporary in the neoclassical perspective, though one could define mismatch as any significant departure from traditional wage differentials across skill groups induced by demand and supply shifts.

As this suggests, economic approaches focus mostly on wage differences by skill as measures of mismatch or shortage, while non-economic conceptions look for more direct or non-wage indicatiors of a discrepancy between the skills workers possess and those employers demand.

The main problem with relying exclusively on wage movements within a supply and demand framework for inferring skills shortages is that wage differentials reflect institutional as well as market forces—variations in rent sharing, for example—rather than skill differences alone, as even some who interpret recent inequality growth in neoclassical terms recognize (Katz and Summers 1989; Katz and Murphy 1992).

The temporal dimension of the skills mismatch issue also generates multiple concepts of mismatch. One can examine how well the skills of the incoming workforce matches the *current* distribution of job skill demands by comparing the personal characteristics of younger cohorts and older cohorts, using educational attainment or test scores, for example. Alternatively, one could accomplish the same thing by comparing young workers' personal characteristics with measures of occupational characteristics of jobs held by older workers, such as DOT ratings—assuming the measures of workers' skills and job skill requirements have comparable metrics.

By extension, performing this exercise using projections of the occupational distribution 10 years from now would indicate whether there is a mismatch between younger workers and the projected future distibution of job skill requirements, an exercise subject to additional uncertainties that surround occupational projections.

It is still another task to compare the skills of the existing or entering workforce with a more ideal job structure relative to the current or projected one. Some argue that the current workforce may be well matched to current and projected skill demands, but that this state of affairs tends to entail more low-skill and low-wage jobs than is socially desirable. Models of low-skill equilibria argue that this depressed level of attainment results from negative and self-reinforcing expectations whereby employers offer mostly low-skill jobs because workers'

skills are limited and job-seekers do not seek more education and training because the available jobs are not structured to utilize them. This
low-skill trap can be overcome only through changes in employer
policy, such as the adoption of higher-value-added production strategies and employee involvement programs, and through more govern-
ment-sponsored training to fill the gaps left by employers (Finegold
1996; Keep and Mayhew 1996). Mainstream economists place more
of the onus for higher attainment on workers, assuming that an increased supply of human capital will create its own demand and raise
wages at the bottom. Either way, these conceptions of mismatch implicitly compare the skills of the current or entering workforce with
the requirements of an improved or ideal job structure, which is usually not specified further.

These three different conceptions of mismatch imply that even if
the skills of workers and jobs could be compared easily, there would
still be a question as to which set of jobs should serve as the reference
point: those in the current, future, or normatively desirable occupational
structure.

Compounding these difficulties, as previous chapters showed, both
the skills possessed by individual workers and those required by individual employers are somewhat flexible in response to differing job and
labor market conditions, making it difficult to specify precisely either a
given job's "requirements" or the workers suitable to hold it.

Mikulecky (1982) is the only study that compares the cognitive abilities of students and workers with workplace skill demands using a common metric—grade-level reading. The sample consisted of urban high
school juniors, adult technical school students, professionals, "mid-level"
workers (clerical, sales, service), and blue-collar workers. The study
was a response to widespread complaints about basic skills deficiencies
in the workforce that were common around the same time *A Nation at
Risk* appeared.

Mikulecky asked study participants to bring in representative reading material from school or work, and he assessed the grade-level difficulty of the school and job reading samples using well-established
readability formulas. Mikulecky also assessed the respondents' own
reading ability using their performance reading both the sample texts
and a newspaper-like text the participants had not seen prior to the
study.

TABLE 6   Comparison of grade-level measures for school and job reading samples and students' and workers' reading performance

	Students		Workers		
	High school	Technical	Professional	Middle	Blue collar
A. Difficulty of school or job sample text	10.6	11.4	11.2	10.9	10.5
Participant reading ability: **B**. School or job text	10.5	11.3	12.6	11.0	11.5
C. New material	10.1	10.8	11.7	10.7	10.8

Source: Mikulecky 1982: 417. Sample drawn from the Indianapolis metropolitan area. Sample size is roughly 50 for all groups. Both groups of students are evenly divided by gender and race (whites and blacks). The employee sample was 63% male, 82% white, 16% black, 2% other race (Mikulecky 1982: 405f.).

The results in **Table 6** show that the average grade-level difficulty of school and job texts are very close to one another (approximately grades 10.5-11) (see Table 6, row A) and the average student and employee in all groups is able to read at or close to that level, whether the text is familiar (row B) or new (row C). Participants' reading performance was also moderately higher (approximately 0.6 grade levels) when the material was more familiar (row B versus row C), as a situated cognition perspective would predict.

In addition, high school students' reading performance on familiar school texts (10.5) was close to the grade-level difficulty of the job samples of the mid-level jobs they were likely to enter (10.9); the reading ability of technical school students (11.3) was higher than the level required by sample materials brought by blue-collar workers (10.5).

Although readability formulae have their methodological limitations, this data provides little evidence of a skills mismatch between either students or current job-holders on the one hand, and job skill requirements on the other. Other studies use either more subjective or indirect measures of mismatch.

Employer surveys

If increased wage inequality since the 1980s does reflect a skills shortage, one might expect employers would show some awareness of it.
Journalistic accounts and employer poll and survey data do suggest firms
have substantial difficulty finding qualified young workers for relatively
routine entry-level positions, at least in urban areas. Most of these accounts reflect the popular themes of public school failure, recent high
school graduates' low basic cognitive skills, and their general lack of
readiness for the world of work (Hull 1991; Hollenbeck 1994; Barton
1990; *Economic Report of the President* 2000, p. 134). For example,
one employer complained, "It's amazing to me how many people can't
multiply and divide" (Hollenbeck 1994, 13f.).

However, difficulties in finding workers with desired social skills,
attitudes, and motivation frequently ranked as high or higher in employers' concerns than dissatisfaction with cognitive skill levels (Hollenbeck
1994; Teixeira 1998; National Association of Manufacturers 2001; Public Agenda 1999; for Britain, see Robinson 1998).

A recent National Association of Manufacturers (NAM) survey found
that most NAM members said the most common reason for rejecting applicants for hourly jobs was poor motivation and work habits (70%), insufficient work experience (34%), and failed drug tests (27%), while cognitive skills deficits—such as poor reading and writing skills (32%), poor
math skills (20%), and poor problem-solving (11%) or technical/com-
puter skills (11%)—were mentioned less often (National Association of
Manufacturers 2001, p. 8). Employers' assessments of the quality of
their own production workers were similar, except that only 60% complained that work habits and motivation were the most serious "skill defi-
ciency" of current employees; less than 15% cited current production
employees' failure to update their skills and education and poor technical/
computer skills as serious problems (National Association of Manufacturers 2001, p. 11). Judging from this survey, an appropriate attitude to
work seems to be the main "skill" in short supply, though it should be
noted that a 1997 NAM survey apparently showed far more complaints
regarding cognitive skill shortfalls.

In recent years, surveys of human resource managers conducted by
the American Management Association (AMA) found that 40% of AMA
member firms test applicants for basic skills, and the average failure

rate is roughly 35%. Approximately 85% of the firms that test do not hire those who fail ("2001 AMA Survey on Workplace Testing: Basic Skills, Job Skills, Psychological Measurement," press release). These findings support the skills mismatch position, but, unlike the NAM survey, the AMA did not ask about motivation and work habits. The AMA says its member firms are larger than average and account for 25% of total national employment, but like all trade association surveys, the sample is not representative of any known population.

A recent national poll of employers by The Public Agenda (1999) found that some two-thirds thought public high school graduates did not have the basic skills needed to succeed, though fewer parents (33%) and students (22%) in parallel surveys felt the same way. A third of employers rated both the writing abilities and work habits of young workers as poor, and a quarter rated math skills as poor, but computer skills ranked close to the bottom of the list of problems (11%). This points to one potential difficulty with the commonplace view that young people are increasingly less prepared for work and that computers are driving the increase in skill requirements; namely, young people are more likely to be computer literate than older workers.

The National Employers Survey (1994) and Rural Manufacturing Survey (RMS) (1996) found the average employer judged 20-25% of its current production or front-line workers not fully proficient at their jobs (National Center on the Educational Quality of the Workforce 1994; Teixeira 1998). This might seem high since the figures refer to workers already matched to jobs and presumably more qualified than the general applicant pool, but the figures also do not control for tenure or age, and there are no historical figures against which to benchmark them. The surveys also contain no information on the size of the applicant pool from which workers were drawn or the percentage of applicants deemed qualified for the positions for which they applied. As noted previously, far fewer employers in the RMS reported major problems finding workers with necessary skills (5-15%) than reported increases in cognitive, computer, and interpersonal skills (Teixeira 1998).

A survey of management and union representatives found only 5% on either side said "pressure to upgrade skills" or the need to negotiate "adjustments to new technology" had a significant role in contracts negotiated between 1993 and 1996. By comparison, roughly 25% of managers mentioned increased domestic competition and pressures on fringe benefits and 15% mentioned falling real wages as significant issues, while 35-45% of union representatives mentioned wages and benefits (Cutcher-Gershenfeld, Kochan, Wells 1998, p. 25).

In their Chicago employer study, Rosenbaum and Binder (1997) reported a substantial skills mismatch between jobs and applicants. Employers complained about the number of young high school grads who could not read or perform math at 8th-grade levels. Roughly 20% of employers said they had to explain tasks in minute detail and assist or closely supervise workers because of their low skills; 45% said they had to simplify job tasks to match employees' low skills. Employers also believed the cognitive skills of recent high school graduates had declined over time and reported they had to simplify tasks to match employees' skills or supervise them more closely than they desired (Rosenbaum and Binder 1997, p. 73). Rosenbaum and Binder conclude that the prevalence of low-skilled jobs reflects a workforce unprepared for more skilled and autonomous work rather than management shortcomings or preferred labor strategies.

However, these employers' judgments that young people's cognitive skills have declined over time are not consistent with national NAEP data. As noted earlier, there are also reasons to be cautious about inferring workers' long-term job abilities from young adults. But Rosenbaum and Binder argue that even if young people compensate for formal skills deficits through situated learning on the job, the skills will be context-bound and inadequate for promotion, though this assumes the jobs have promotion opportunities requiring more formally acquired skills.

Crain's study of employers of NLS72 respondents finds that 48% of employers reported that they sometimes find high school graduates do not have the reading and math skills needed to be hired, but only 6% provided basic skills training to fill this gap, consistent with the CPS results mentioned previously. In contrast to Rosenbaum and Binder's findings, only 2% of employers said they have "often found it necessary to redesign or simplify the reading or math requirements of jobs because of weaknesses of our workers in these areas" (Crain 1984, p. 25).

Econometric studies

Most economists infer an increased scarcity of human capital from the fact that the relative wages of college graduates increased in the 1980s even as their relative supply increased, though there is no consensus on whether the cause was an acceleration of demand for skills—perhaps as a result of the spread of computers—or a deceleration in the growth of the supply of skills as a result of the post-Vietnam drop in college attendance (Katz and Murphy 1992; Autor et al. 1998; Danziger and Gottschalk 1995; Gottschalk and Smeeding 1997; Levy and Murnane 1996; Card and Lemieux 2001).

Based mostly on analyses of data from the 1980s, this view has not developed a consensus account of the general stability of wage inequality in the 1990s, when macroeconomic conditions improved considerably but the growth in educational attainment moderated and investment in computers and other information technology remained strong. Several studies of job loss in the 1990s found that more educated white-collar workers experienced the greatest increase in job displacement and insecurity, contrary to the notion that such workers are increasingly scarce (Farber 1997; Aaronson and Sullivan 1998; Schmidt 1999). It is possible that this white-collar job loss signifies that some of the growth of managerial and professional employment in the 1980s represented overhiring that was subject to later correction or perhaps indicates an extension of the same lean-staffing and work-intensification principles from blue-collar to white-collar workers.

Some researchers even believe that the oversupply of college graduates detected in the 1970s persisted into the 1980s, a decade when most economists believe an acute shortage of college graduates raised the college/high-school wage differential. Hecker (1992, p. 4) found that the percentage of college grads either in occupations not requiring a college degree or unemployed rose from 12% (1967) to 18.6% (1980) and continued to rise modestly to 19.9% during the years of ostensible shortage (1990).[5] Furthermore, the supply of college graduates grew 62% between 1979 and 1990, while total employment in managerial, professional, technical, and other high-skilled occupations grew only 57% (Hecker 1992, p. 7).

Hecker noted that wage inequality during the 1980s resulted more from declining real wages for males with high school degrees (or less) than from increases in real wages for college graduates, and he concluded that sectoral shifts from manufacturing to services was a more likely cause of inequality growth than a shortage of college-educated workers. BLS research also did not uncover evidence that employers wanted to hire more college graduates at current wages than they actually hired. Hecker concluded that even greater increases in the supply of college graduates in the 1980s would have only increased the number of underutilized college-educated workers, though he recognizes that college graduates in occupations that do not require college degrees receive higher wages than high school graduates in those occupations (Hecker 1992, p. 11).

In response to Hecker's research, Tyler et al. (1995) uphold the mainstream skills shortage view by showing that the problem of college-educated workers in non-college jobs in the 1980s was increasingly a problem for older males compared to other groups. They attributed this to restructuring and downsizing in the 1980s, which harmed the employment prospects even of well-educated older workers.

However, it is notable that the numbers of college-educated workers employed in traditionally non-college jobs remained high throughout the 1980s, despite the ostensible shortage of college-educated workers. Balancing this somewhat is the argument that because the high school-college wage differential increased even within non-college jobs, computers may have raised the skill demands of some of these jobs from non-college to college level (Boesel and Fredland 1999, 22ff.).

Another problem with most economic studies is that they do not identify the specific skills believed to be in short supply, though the general view seems to be that it is higher-level cognitive skills associated with college graduates that are most scarce. By contrast, none of the other literature reviewed here found employers complaining much about a shortage of college-educated workers or their high wages, and even concern with computer skills was limited. Employers complain almost exclusively about the work attitudes and basic skills of non-college workers.

Using test scores rather than education as the measure of skills, Murnane et al. (1995) delved somewhat deeper into the issue of the specific skills in short supply. They found that the wage differential associated with a standard deviation in math test scores for 24-year old workers rose from roughly 2.5% to 6.9% for males and from 5.6% to 10.6% for females between 1978 and 1986, controlling for education and other variables (calculated from Murnane et al. 1995, 257ff.). Controlling for occupation indicates that most of the effect is within occupations, rather than due to the changing occupational composition of the workforce.

However, in their interpretation of the results, the authors are somewhat inconsistent as to whether it is math skills *per se* that are increasingly rewarded, or cognitive skills more generally, for which the math scores are simply good proxies (Murnane et al. 1995, 259f.). They cite the NAEP data using performance categories to suggest that only about half the nation's high school seniors have 8th-grade math skills, such as the ability to understand decimals, fractions, and line graphs. The implication seems to be that employers value these basic skills specifically, though this differs from much of the economic literature, which emphasizes growing demand for college graduates. Though plausible, there really is no evidence on the specific math skills demanded by employers other than Smith (1999), and work reviewed above suggests that the descriptions of NAEP performance levels have validity problems and cannot be taken at face value. In addition, NAEP reading scores for a sample of 21 to 25 year olds show that 80% read above the 8th-grade average in 1985 (Kirsch and Jungeblut 1986, p. 40).

Even Murnane et al.'s study showed that the highest-scoring males in 1986 earned less than the lowest-scoring males in 1978, and the situation was nearly the same for females, suggesting that more is at work than just changing returns to skills. The whole structure of wages seems to have shifted downward and this effect appears to be larger than the changing returns to test scores. Murnane et al. acknowledge that "helping a male graduating from high school in 1980 to improve his math skills would contribute only modestly to the goal of increasing his wage level at age 24 to the level enjoyed by males graduating eight years earlier" (1995, p. 260).

In addition, Bowles and Gintis contest Murnane et al.'s basic finding. Reviewing 65 estimates from different periods across numerous studies, they find no trend in tests scores' effects on earnings, in the proportion of the returns to education they explain, or in their increment to R^2 (Bowles and Gintis 2002).

Cross-sectional comparative studies using the International Adult Literacy Survey cast more serious doubt on test scores and inequality in cognitive skills as the explanation for the high levels of U.S. wage inequality. They find that greater inequality of cognitive skills in the United States does not explain much of the higher U.S. earnings inequality relative to European countries (Devroye and Freeman 2001; Blau and Kahn 2001).

Devroye and Freeman (2001) find that the United States has greater earnings inequality and greater adult test score inequality than three European countries with similar data (Germany, Netherlands, and Sweden). However, if the United States had the same distribution of scores as those countries, earnings inequality in the United States and the difference in inequality between the United States and the other countries would decline only marginally. Two-thirds of the difference in earnings inequality between the U.S. and the other countries is within test score groups. In fact, the standard deviation of earnings among U.S. workers with the *same* test scores is greater than the standard deviation of earnings for *all* workers in the European countries. Blau and Kahn (2001, p. 20) draw similar conclusions from analyses of the IALS that compare the United States to Canada, Switzerland, the Netherlands, and Sweden.

This research suggests some of the limits of explaining wage inequality based on variation in cognitive skills. Clearly, institutional changes within the United States over time and differences between the United States and other countries are important in explaining the high levels of U.S. inequality. Observed wage differentials are not simply the returns to human capital that result from the operation of universal market forces.

Studies of welfare-to-work and other disadvantaged groups

Another unexpected finding that casts doubt on some skills mismatch arguments is the remarkable employment rate among the large number of women exiting the welfare rolls since the mid-1990s. Most observers did not foresee this development and many believed that low skills in this group would be a much more serious barrier to employment.

Holzer found in his first survey of employers for the MCSUI project (1992-94) that even most low-skill jobs required reading, math, and other cognitive skills, and he worried that with welfare reform, "it seems highly probable that the imbalance between job availability and the number of people with low skills and credentials that already exists in many central-city areas will worsen over the next few years" (Holzer 1996, p. 70).

Even a recent review of the welfare-to-work literature written at the peak of the late 1990s boom asserted, "There is a large gap between the skills that employers demand and those welfare recipients can offer." The review cited the low NALS scores of welfare recipients as supporting evidence, including the familiar claim that those scoring at Level 2 are unable to use a bus schedule (Corcoran et al. 2000, 255f.).

The actual employment record of former welfare recipients does not support these dire predictions. Recent research indicates that roughly 75% of former recipients work at some point in the year after leaving welfare, usually full-time, and roughly 30% of current welfare recipients are employed, despite their low levels of education (Moffitt 2002). In the 20 largest metropolitan areas, the employment-to-population ratio of all single mothers rose from 59% in 1995-96, the year before national welfare reform, to 73% three years later in 1998-99, a large jump that presumably reflects changes in welfare programs to a significant degree. There also appears to be no association between the increasing labor force participation of single mothers and the employment or wage rates of other less-educated workers, suggesting that the increased employment of former welfare recipients did not represent simply substitution of these workers for others who were displaced (Lerman and Ratcliffe 2001).

Holzer's subsequent four-city survey (1998) found that the percentage of former welfare recipients in jobs requiring daily reading, writing, math, and computer use was only somewhat below that observed for all non-college workers in his first survey (see **Table 7**) (Holzer and Stoll 2001). What is remarkable is not how cognitively demanding most less-skilled jobs are, but how easily those presumably ranking low in the skills distribution can fill them. Either the skills of welfare recipients were underestimated, the demands of jobs overestimated, or the method for comparing the two has problems (such as the coarseness of skill categories, for example).

It is possible that the tight labor market of the late 1990s forced employers to take on lower-quality workers than they would otherwise hire, while at the same time welfare reform forced many women into the labor market. However, Holzer's recent survey provides little support for this conclusion, at least with respect to cognitive skills. Only about 10% of employers reported that former welfare recipients had problems with basic and job-related skills, and only 10-20% rated them worse overall than their other employees in similar jobs. Employers most frequently cited problems with absenteeism related to child care (63%), transportation difficulties (44%), and physical health problems (32%) (Holzer and Stoll 2001).

TABLE 7 Percentage of all non-college jobs and jobs filled by former welfare recipients that required performing different tasks daily

	All jobs	Jobs held by former welfare recipients				
	4 cities	Average	LA	Chicago	Cleveland	Milwaukee
Read paragraphs	55					
Write paragraphs	30					
Read/write		56	62	50	56	52
Arithmetic	65	54	58	50	51	58
Use computers	51	44	52	36	40	41
Serve customers	58	78	83	70	68	99

Note: Figures for four-city survey are averages for Los Angeles, Detroit, Boston, and Atlanta (1992-94). Figures for other cities are from 1998. Average is weighted by population (Holzer and Stoll 2001).

Source: Holzer (1996: 49) and Holzer and Stoll (2001: Table 4.2).

Of course, these employers were referring to job incumbents, not the overall pool of former welfare recipients, so there is the possibility of selection effects. The workers they hired were not a random sample of all former welfare recipients. However, the large number of women exiting the rolls and finding employment suggests that creaming is unlikely to explain all of Holzer's results.

This inference is confirmed by another survey that does not suffer from selection problems. Johnson and Corcoran (2002) surveyed a random sample of people receiving welfare in an urban Michigan county in early 1997 and re-surveyed them in 1998 and again in 1999, when many had left the welfare rolls. Unlike Holzer and Stoll (2001), this study followed a random sample of people initially receiving welfare, including those remaining on the welfare rolls or unemployed in later years. The study also differentiated employment into "good" jobs and "bad" jobs, with good jobs defined as full-time and either paying $7 per hour and providing health benefits or paying $8.50 without health benefits. Consistent with other studies, Johnson and Corcoran found that roughly 70% of the people in their welfare sample were employed shortly after their first survey, with roughly 50% in bad jobs (**Table 8**, right panel, bottom row).

TABLE 8   Skills employers required for recently-filled non-college jobs in 1997 and the job skills of those who received welfare in 1997 by employment status in 1998-1999 (percentage of jobs requiring or people possessing skill)

| | Skills jobs require (employer survey 1997) | | | Skills possessed by job-holders and unemployed in 1998-99 (survey of 1997 welfare recipients) | | | |
	All	Good jobs	Bad jobs	All	Good job	Bad job	Unemployed
Read/write	41.6%	49.1%	35.4%	52.0%	70.3%	51.0%	40.5%
Arithmetic	62.8	68.2	58.4	60.3	65.9	66.8	45.2
Computers	43.7	48.6	39.6	26.1	42.2	24.7	17.0
Customers	63.4	54.2	70.9	72.6	69.5	82.7	57.4
None	14.8	13.7	15.7	14.5	8.4	9.4	27.7
Percent of sample	100%	45%	55%	100%	21%	50%	29%

Note: Employer survey covered three metropolitan areas in Michigan, survey of former welfare recipients covered an urban Michigan county. Good jobs were defined as full-time and either paying at least $7 per hour and offering health benefits or paying at least $8.50 per hour and not offering health benefits.

Source: Johnson and Corcoran (2002).

The study asked respondents whether they had performed five tasks on a daily basis in any previous job they held: reading and writing of paragraph-length material, arithmetic use, computer use, and customer contact. These measures of workers' job skills can be compared to job skill requirements in their region from an independent survey of local employers asking about daily performance of the same five tasks for recently filled non-college jobs. As with Mikulecky (1982), this is one of the few studies that permits comparisons of workers' skills and job skill requirements using the same yardstick.

Results for the full sample (Table 8, column 4) indicate that the skills of people receiving welfare in 1997 were roughly in line with the skills demanded by employers for all non-college jobs (column 1) and not too different from those demanded by good jobs (column 2), with the notable exception of computer experience. For example, 41.6% of all jobs required daily reading and writing and 52.0% of welfare recipients in 1997 reported that they had worked in a job requiring daily reading and writing at some point.

Remarkably, even those in bad jobs (column 6) seem to have cognitive skills in roughly the same proportions as required by good jobs, except for computer experience. Not surprisingly, the job skills reportedly used by those who remained unemployed when re-surveyed (column 7) are the lowest of the three groups, though the percentage of the sample in this category (29%) was not large enough to depress the overall averages below the levels required by employers, except in the case of computer use.

As a caveat to the preceding, one should note that it is a little misleading to simply compare percentages across the employer and worker surveys because they are calculated on different base populations. Without further information on absolute population magnitudes, there is no real way to know if there is an imbalance between job requirements and workers' skills.

For example, suppose the percentages in the left panel of Table 8 refer to a population of, say, 100,000 jobs and the percentages in the right panel refer to a population of, say, 30,000 welfare recipients. In this case the large percentage of job seekers without computer skills (75%) relative to the smaller percentage of jobs not requiring such skills (56%) implies only 22,500 job seekers without computer experience compared to 56,000 jobs that do not require computer skills. Whether or not there is actually a mismatch of worker skills and job requirements with respect to computer skills depends on both the absolute number of job seekers and jobs, as well as the percentage of each having or requiring the skill.

Of course, former welfare recipients also have to compete with other low-skilled job seekers for these positions, which further complicates the issue of whether a mismatch exists. Nevertheless, Johnson and Corcoran (2002) is the only study that compares the skills of a representative sample of welfare recipients with the skills required by low-skill jobs and finds remarkably few differences between the two.

A further limitation of both Holzer's studies (1996; Holzer and Stoll 2001) and Johnson and Corcoran's study (2002) is that the skill measures are fairly coarse. Consequently, there is no way to know whether the level of complexity of the different tasks performed by welfare recipients in prior jobs was comparable to the levels employers said they require. However, the high employment rates among former welfare recipients at prevailing wages and the high levels of employers' reported satisfaction with their cognitive skills suggest that job seekers were successfully matched with jobs at high rates.

This is not to say that skills do not matter. The right panel of Table 8 shows clearly that employment and job quality is positively associated with experience using different job-related skills. Analyses by Danziger et al. (1999) confirm that both education and previous use of the job skills in Table 8 affect the probability of employment among former welfare recipients, as do non-cognitive problems, such as physical and mental health, transportation difficulties, and perceived discrimination in prior jobs. In fact, all have roughly comparable effects.[6]

In addition, employment alone is not the only important outcome measure. Holzer and Stoll (2001) report a median wage of $7 per hour in 1998 for those with jobs. This was about $2 above the minimum wage, indicating that employers were willing to pay these workers more than what was legally required, but clearly the wages were low and health insurance was also uncommon. This partly explains workers' weak attachment to these jobs and the job churning that is often observed in welfare-to-work studies. In fact, resignations outnumber dismissals by two to one as a cause of job churning among former welfare recipients, suggesting that employees' dissatisfaction and personal problems are the more pertinent factors in employment instability, rather than employer dissatisfaction with cognitive skill deficits, though low education and skills are also associated with unstable employment (Campbell et al. 2002).

The low pay and probable dependence of many such jobs on a strong business cycle (Holzer, Raphael, and Stoll 2003, 30ff.) confirm that these low-skilled workers are found disproportionately at the bottom of the job hierarchy and remain vulnerable. Former welfare recipients usually fill jobs in the secondary labor market. However, it is not accurate to say that their low skills shut them out of the labor market. Their recent experience in the job market is no better than many other less-skilled workers, but in many respects does not seem worse. Given favorable conditions, most can be integrated into the existing job skill structure. The absence of better-paid employment partly reflects structural shifts in the kinds of jobs the economy generates, as well as possible limits to the kinds of jobs these workers can perform. The experience of former welfare recipients in the late 1990s underscores the importance of a strong macroeconomy and the availability of jobs in determining labor market outcomes, rather than individuals' skills alone (Galbraith 1998).

Nevertheless, even a strong macroeconomy did not lift the fortunes of everyone at the lower end of the skill distribution. The unemployment rate for less-educated young black males remained stubbornly above the rate for similar whites (Holzer and Offner 2002), but whether this reflects human capital differences is much debated. Several studies show that adding Armed Forces Qualification Test (AFQT) scores to a standard human capital model greatly reduces black-white wage differences in the cross-section (Neal and Johnson 1996; Farkas and Vicknair 1996). Others contend that the test is racially biased and that after scores are adjusted, evidence of greater discrimination reemerges (Maume et al. 1996; Moss and Tilly 2001, 76f.). Even assuming the same results hold for differences in employment rates, it is not clear how either of these cross-sectional claims can account for the flat employment trend in the tight labor market of the late 1990s.

Moss and Tilly's interviews with employers shed further light on the question of the extent to which black males' recent labor market experience reflects lack of human capital or the effects of discrimination. They found that many employers did complain of cognitive skill deficits among black males, but many also indicated the jobs required little more than reliability and common courtesy and complained more often about motivation and attitude problems, and almost as much about interactional styles (Moss and Tilly 2001, 59f.). When comparing black males to other groups, employers viewed black women and especially Hispanics and Asians more positively on these "soft skills," often citing the latter groups' immigrant work ethic (Moss and Tilly 2001, Chapter 4). Moss and Tilly (2001, 142ff., p. 154) conclude that employers' perceptions are some combination of false stereotypes, cultural gaps, and true differences between black males and other groups, the latter partly reflecting native-born black males' dissatisfaction with the poor wages and working conditions of the jobs available to them relative to other native-born Americans, which comprise their reference group. What employers praised in other groups was often a willingness to work hard in the least desirable jobs, many of which were unattractive both to whites and to native-born blacks, but which immigrant minorities accepted more readily because their reference points were even poorer jobs in their country of origin (Moss and Tilly 2001, 117ff.).

Although Moss and Tilly's study cannot assign proportions to the different forces they identify, it is clear that the employment difficulties of black males are more complex than simply an issue of cognitive skills.

Summary

Employers do complain about the difficulty of meeting their labor needs with the workforce available to them, but it is not clear if those concerns focus more on workers' attitudes than on their cognitive skills, nor whether that concern applies to many groups beyond young workers, for whom many of the problems may in any case be transitory. Employers have few complaints regarding the scarcity, expense, or skill levels of workers with more than a high school education, contrary to the preoccupation of most of the labor economics literature on wage inequality growth. There is no consistent historical data against which to benchmark the current levels of expressed dissatisfaction among employers.

The increased rewards associated with education and test scores suggest human capital shortages, but they may also be a proxy for other institutional shifts. Test scores do not explain much of the unusually high levels of wage inequality in the United States compared to continental Europe. The stability of U.S. inequality and education differentials in the 1990s is also hard to reconcile with a simple supply and demand story, given the absence of large increases in the supply of human capital and the presumably steady increase in demand as information technology diffused further in the workplace.

Despite the increased returns to education in the last 20 years, the experience of former welfare recipients shows there is room in the labor market for large numbers of even very low-skilled workers, at least under favorable macroeconomic conditions, though the low wages in these secondary-sector jobs remain a problem.

Conclusion

Firm conclusions about the alleged skills mismatch are hampered by three problems: difficulties in ascertaining the job-relevant skills workers possess, an even more striking scarcity of information on the skills their jobs require, and problems relating the two kinds of evidence to one another. Both workers and employers have a certain flexibility in the skills they can develop on the job or require for a given job, which means that flexible ranges of worker abilities can be matched to flexible ranges of jobs in actual labor markets. The available research results do not speak with one voice, but certain conclusions seem reasonable.

There is little evidence of absolute declines in cognitive or hard skills in the United States, nor of generally poor performance relative to other advanced industrialized countries, despite frequent extreme statements to the contrary in popular and policy circles. Test score differences between the United States and other industrialized countries are related to different patterns of immigration and assimilation, which often reflect U.S. employer preferences for low-skill, low-wage workers, rather than a significant skills gap. However, there is also evidence of decelerating growth of human capital and of stability in cognitive test scores. Since skill demands appear to be gradually rising, lack of stronger growth in the supply of human capital may be a problem, but this cannot be known without better information than is currently available on the actual level of job skill requirements and whether they really push more jobs out of reach for different subgroups at current wage rates. It is even unclear how much of the purported skills mismatch problem is a shortage of cognitive skills rather than an expression of employer dissatisfaction with effort levels or work-related attitudes, and whether any such problem extends beyond a transitory stage of young adulthood and/or some fraction of disadvantaged minorities.

As for computer skills, research findings in the skills mismatch literature do not suggest these skills are in particularly short supply, despite the technology focus of much of this debate, nor is there evidence of a general shortage of other technical or high-level skills. Even claims of accelerating demand for college graduates more generally do not resonate with employers.

And in many cases, the lack of historical data makes it impossible to know whether recent levels of expressed dissatisfaction are higher than in the past.

A key question is whether policies to increase human capital are the solution to the problem of high wage inequality and low wages for some groups. The goals of increasing achievement in elementary and secondary schools and raising postsecondary enrollment are worthy, but the pursuit of those goals has tended to generate heated debate over methods (vouchers, for example, or high-stakes testing) and exaggerated claims regarding the problems with public schools and the expected outcomes of proposed reforms.

Raising everyone's absolute cognitive skills and work readiness will not increase wages and decrease inequality if wages are determined by the structure of jobs and one's relative position in the worker queue (Thurow 1975). An implicit view holds that increasing the supply of skill will satisfy pent-up demand or perhaps create its own demand. However, education levels grew at an exceptional rate in the late 1960s-70s and merely depressed the college premium. At exactly the time when unprecedented numbers of highly educated workers entered the workforce, the overall wage level entered a 25-year period of stagnation, ending an equally long period of unprecedented growth between 1948 and 1972. Increasing levels of human capital at the bottom is desirable for many reasons, but recent changes in the wage structure may not reflect human capital scarcities as much as management strategies. Wages may be more responsive to institutional reforms that more directly affect compensation or economic activity—measures such as maintaining the value of the minimum wage, union protections, and strong macroeconomic growth—than to changes in education or skill levels.

Finally, one way to answer some of the many questions raised by the skills mismatch debate is to develop more detailed and standardized measures for tracking trends in job skill requirements, and to apply these measures consistently to representative samples of workers over time in order to understand exactly how work is changing, rather than trying to infer changes from the very limited information currently available.

Endnotes

1.   Traditional views of intelligence hold that skills gained through experience are: imperfect substitutes for more formally acquired skills or pre-existing abilities; overly context-bound and tied to concrete actions; and unlikely to generalize or transfer to new situations (Gottfredson 1997). Even some observers sympathetic to the situated cognition perspective believe that work with computers requires procedural reasoning and more explicit, abstract, and conceptual knowledge, in addition to formal instruction and on-the-job experience (Zuboff 1988).

2.   This sample includes three countries/regions (France, Italy, Northern Ireland) for which tabulations are not presented in the main IALS report (OECD and Statistics Canada 2000).

3.   Data from the Netherlands were not available when the main PISA was published (OECD 2001, p. 13) and eastern Germans did not participate in the IALS.

4.   Respondents were allowed to give more than one reason for needing new job skills in the previous 12 months.

5.   Hecker (1992, p. 4) classifies the following jobs as not requiring a college degree based on BLS surveys: retail sales, clerical and other administrative support, craft, operator, laborer, service occupations, and farm worker, excluding insurance adjusters and investigators, craft supervisors, police officers, and farm managers.

6.   Of course, education may also affect the likelihood of suffering from physical or mental health problems and thus indirectly affect the probability of employment even for jobs with low cognitive skill requirements.

Bibliography

Aaronson, Daniel and Daniel G. Sullivan. 1998. "The Decline of Job Security in the 1990s: Displacement, Anxiety, and Their Effect on Wage Growth." *Economic Perspectives*. 22 (1): 17-43.

Alwin, Duane F. 1991. "Family of Origin and Cohort Differences in Verbal Ability." *American Sociological Review*. 56: 625-638.

Alwin, Duane F. and Ryan J. McCammon. 1999. "Aging versus cohort interpretations of intercohort differences in GSS vocabulary scores." *American Sociological Review*. 67: 272-86.

Applebome, Paul. 1995. "Employers Wary of School System." *New York Times*. February 20, 1995: A13.

Attewell, Paul. 1987. "The Deskilling Controversy." *Work and Occupations*. 14: 323-346.

Attewell, Paul. 1990. "What is skill?" *Work and Occupations*. 17: 422-48.

Autor, David H., Lawrence F. Katz, and Alan B. Krueger. 1998. "Computing Inequality: Have Computers Changed the Labor Market?" *Quarterly Journal of Economics*. 113: 1169-1213.

Bailey, Thomas R. and Annette D. Bernhardt. 1997. "In Search of the High Road in a Low-wage Industry." *Politics and Society*. 25: 179-201.

Barton, Paul E. 1990. "Skill Employers Need: Time to Measure Them?" Princeton, NJ: Education Testing Service.

Barton, Paul E. 2000. "What Jobs Require: Literacy, Education, and Training, 1940-2006." Princeton, NJ: Education Testing Service.

Bell, Daniel. 1976. *The Coming of Post-industrial Society: A Venture in Social Forecasting*. New York: Basic Books.

Bills, David B. 1992a. "The Mutability of Educational Credentials as Hiring Criteria." *Work and Occupations*. 19: 79-95.

Bills, David B. 1992b. "A Survey of Employer Surveys: What We Know About Labor Markets From Talking With Bosses." *Research in Social Stratification and Mobility*. 11: 3-31.

Bishop, John H. 1989. "Is the Test Score Decline Responsible for the Productivity Growth Decline?" *American Economic Review*. 79: 178-97.

Bishop, John H. 1991. "Achievement, Test Scores, and Relative Wages." pp.146-186 in *Workers and Their Wages*, Marvin H. Kosters, ed. Washington, DC: AEI Press.

Blau, Francine D. and Lawrence M. Kahn. 2001. "Do Cognitive Test Scores Explain Higher U.S. Wage Inequality?" National Bureau of Economic Research Working Paper 8210. Cambridge, MA.

Boesel, David and Eric Fredland. 1999. "College for All? Is There Too Much Emphasis on Getting a 4-Year College Degree?" National Library of Education. Washington, DC: U.S. Department of Education.

Booth, Alison L. and Dennis J. Snower. 1996. *Acquiring Skills: Market Failures, Their Symptoms, and Policy Responses.* Cambridge: Cambridge University Press.

Borman, Walter C., Mary Ann Hanson, and Jerry W. Hedge. 1997. "Personnel Selection." *Annual Review of Psychology.* 48: 299-337.

Bowles, Samuel and Herbert Gintis. 1976. *Schooling in Capitalist America.* New York: Basic Books.

Bowles, Samuel and Herbert Gintis. 2002. "*Schooling in Capitalist America* Revisited." *Sociology of Education.* 75: 1-18.

Bresnahan, Timothy F., Erik Brynjolfsson, Loren M. Hitt. 2002. "Information Technology, Workplace Organization, and the Demand for Skilled Labor: Firm-Level Evidence." *Quarterly Journal of Economics.* 117: 339-76.

Cain, Glenn G. 1976. "The Challenge of Segmented Labor Market Theories to Orthodox Theory: A Survey." *Journal of Economic Literature.* 14: 1215-57.

Cain, Pamela S. and Donald J. Treiman. 1981. "The *Dictionary of Occupational Titles* as a Source of Occupational Data." *American Sociological Review.* 46: 253-78.

California Workforce Literacy Task Force. 1991. "California's Workforce for the Year 2000." Study papers of the California Workforce Literacy Task Force.

Campbell, Jay R., Catherine M. Hombo, John Mazzeo. 2000. *Trends in Academic Progress: Three Decades of Student Performance.* National Center for Educational Statistics. Washington, DC: U.S. Department of Education.

Campbell, Nancye, John K. Maniha, and Howard Roslston. 2002. "Job Retention and Advancement in Welfare Reform." Policy Brief 18. Washington, DC: Brookings Institution.

Cappelli, Peter. 1995. "Is the 'Skills Gap' Really About Attitudes?" *California Management Review.* 37: 108-124.

Carbonaro, W. 2002. "Skill Mismatches in the 'New Economy': The Importance of Skill Demands for Earnings and Returns to Skill." Paper presented at the Annual Meeting of the American Sociological Association, Chicago IL.

Card, David and Thomas Lemieux. 2001. "Can Falling Supply Explain the Rising Return to College for Younger Men? A Cohort-Based Analysis." *Quarterly Journal of Economics.* 116: 705-46.

Ceci, Stephen J., Jeffrey Liker. "Academic and Nonacademic Intelligence: An Experimental Separation." See Sternberg and Wagner, pp.119-42.

Cohn Elchanan and Shahina P. Khan. 1995. "The Wage Effects of Overschooling Revisited." *Labour Economics.* 2: 67-76.

Constantine, Jill and David Neumark. "Training and the Growth of Wage Inequality." *Industrial Relations.* 35: 491-510.

Corcoran, Mary, Sandra K. Danziger, Ariel Kalil, and Kristin S. Seefeldt. 2000. "How Welfare Reform is Affecting Women's Work." *Annual Review of Sociology.* 26: 241-269.

Crain, Robert L. 1984. "The Quality of American High School Graduates: What Personnel Officers Say and do About It." Report No. 354. Center for the Social Organization of Schools. Johns Hopkins University.

Cutcher-Gershenfeld, Joel, Thomas A. Kochan, and John Calhoun Wells. 1998. "How Do Labor and Management View Collective Bargaining?" *Monthly Labor Review.* October: 23-31.

Daly, Mary C., Felix Büchel, and Greg J. Duncan. 2000. "Premiums and Penalties for Surplus and Deficit Education: Evidence from the United States and Germany." *Economics of Education Review.* 19: 169-78.

Danziger, Sandra, Mary Corcoran, Sheldon Danziger, Colleen Heflin, Ariel Kalil, Judith Levine, Daniel Rosen, Kristin Seefeldt, Kristine Siefert, Richard Tolman. 1999. "Barriers to the Employment of Welfare Recipients." Poverty Research and Training Center, University of Michigan. Also published in *Prosperity For All?: The Economic Boom and African Americans* (2000), Robert Cherry and William M. Rodgers III, eds. New York: Russell Sage.

Danziger, Sheldon and Peter Gottschalk. 1995. *America Unequal.* Cambridge, MA: Harvard University Press.

Devereux, Paul J. 2000. "Task Assignment over the Business Cycle." *Journal of Labor Economics.* 18: 98-124.

Devroye, Daniel, Richard B. Freeman. 2001. "Does Inequality in Skills Explain Inequality of Earnings Across Advanced Countries?" National Bureau of Economic Research. Working Paper 8140. Cambridge, MA.

DiNardo, John E., Nicole M. Fortin, Thomas Lemieux. 1996. "Labor Market Institutions and the Distribution of Wages, 1973-1992: A Semiparametric Approach." *Econometrica.* 64: 1001-44.

Duncan, Greg J., Saul Hoffman. 1981. "The Incidence and Wage Effects of Overeducation." *Economics of Education Review.* 1: 75-86.

Eliason, Scott R. 1995. "An Extension of the Sorensen-Kalleberg Theory of the Labor Market Matching and Attainment Processes." *American Sociological Review.* 60: 247-71.

Farber, Henry S. 1997. "The Changing Face of Job Loss in the United States, 1981-1995." *Brookings Papers on Economic Activity, Microeconomics.* 1997: 55-128.

Farkas, George and Vicknair, Keven. 1996. "Appropriate Tests of Racial Wage Discrimination Require Controls for Cognitive Skill: Comment on Cancio, Evans, and Maume." *American Sociological Review.* 61: 557-60.

Fernandez, Roberto M. 2001. "Skill-Biased Technological Change and Wage Inequality: Evidence from a Plant Retooling." *American Sociological Review*. 107: 273-320.

Finegold, David. 1996. "Market Failure and Government Failure in Skills Investment." See Booth and Snower 1996, pp. 235-53.

Form, William. 1987. "On the Degradation of Skills." *Annual Review of Sociology*. 13: 29-47.

Flynn, James R. 1998. "IQ Gains Over Time: Toward Finding the Causes." See Neisser 1998, pp.25-66.

Freeman, Richard B. and Ronald Schettkat. 2001. "Skill Compression, Wage Differentials, and Employment: Germany vs. the US." *Oxford Economic Papers*. 53: 582-603.

French, Howard W. 2001. "More Sunshine for Japan's Overworked Students." *New York Times*. February 25, 2001: 6.

Friedberg, Leora. 2001. "The Impact of Technological Change on Older Workers: Evidence from Data on Computer Use." Working Paper No. 8297. Cambridge, MA: National Bureau of Economic Research.

Galbraith, James K. 1998. *Created Unequal: The Crisis in American Pay*. New York: Free Press.

Gardner, Peter H., Nik Chmiel, and Toby D. Wall. 1996. "Implicit Knowledge and Fault Diagnosis in the Control of Advanced Manufacturing Technology." *Behaviour and Information Technology*. 15: 205-12.

Glenn, Norval D. "Further Discussion of the Evidence for an Intercohort Decline in Education-Adjusted Vocabulary." 1999. *American Sociological Review*. 64: 267-71.

Gogan, Janis L. 1994. "Motorola-Elma." Harvard Business School Case N9-494-136.

Goode, Erich and Nachman Ben-Yehuda. 1994. "Moral Panics: Culture, Politics, and Social Construction." *Annual Review of Sociology*. 20: 149-71.

Gottfredson, Linda S. 1997. "Why *g* Matters: The Complexity of Everyday Life." *Intelligence*. 24: 79-132.

Gottschalk, Peter and Timothy M. Smeeding. 1997. "Cross-National Comparisons of Earnings and Income Inequality." *Journal of Economic Literature*. 35: 633-87.

Graham, Laurie. 1993. "Inside a Japanese Transplant: A Critical Perspective." *Work and Occupations*. 20: 147-73.

Handel, Michael J. 2000. *Models of Economic Organization and the New Inequality in the United States*. Ph.D. dissertation: Harvard University.

Handel, Michael J. 2003. "Implications of Information Technologies for Employment, Skills, and Wages: A Review of Recent Research." SRI International. Arlington, VA. Available at http://www.sri.com/policy/csted/reports/sandt/it/.

Handel, Michael J. and David I. Levine. 2004. "The Effects of New Work Practices on Workers" *Industrial Relations.* 43: 1-43.

Harrison, Bennett and Barry Bluestone. 1988. *The Great U-Turn: Corporate Restructuring and the Polarizing of America.* New York: Basic Books.

Hartigan, John A. and Alexandra K. Wigdor, eds. 1989. *Fairness in Employment Testing: Validity Generalization, Minority Issues, and the General Aptitude Test Battery.* Washington, DC: National Academy Press.

Hauser, Robert M. 1998. "Trends in Black-White Test Score Differentials: Uses and Misuses of NAEP/SAT Data. See Neisser 1998, pp. 219-49.

Hauser, Robert M. and Min-Hsiung Huang. 1997. "Verbal Ability and Socio-Economic Status: A Trend Analysis." *Social Science Research.* 26: 331-76.

Henning, M, Krzemien G, Myers-Reitmeier J. 1992. "ECC Occupational Analysis and Literacy Audit: Motorola, Inc." Unpublished.

Hecker, Daniel E. 1992. "Reconciling Conflicting Data on Jobs for College Graduates." *Monthly Labor Review.* July: 3-12.

Hollenbeck, Kevin. 1994. "The Workplace Know-How Skills Needed to be Productive." Kalamazoo, MI: W.E. Upjohn Institute.

Holzer, Harry J. 1996. *What Employers Want: Job Prospects for Less Educated Workers.* New York: Russell Sage.

Holzer, Harry J. and Paul Offner. 2002. "Trends in Employment Outcomes of Young Black Men, 1979-2000." Discussion Paper no. 1247-02. Madison, WI: Institute for Research on Poverty.

Holzer, Harry J., Steven Raphael, and Michael A. Stoll. 2003. "Employers in the Boom: How Did the Hiring of Unskilled workers Change during the 1990s?" Discussion Paper no. 1267-03. Madison, WI: Institute for Research on Poverty.

Holzer, Harry J. and Michael A. Stoll. 2001. "Employers and Welfare Recipients: The Effects of Welfare Reform in the Workplace." San Francisco, CA: Public Policy Institute of California.

Howell, David R. 1997. "Institutional Failure and the American Worker: The Collapse of Low-Skill Wages." Public Policy Brief 29. Jerome Levy Economics Institute.

Howell, David R. and Edward N. Wolff. 1991. "Trends in the Growth and Distribution of Skills in the U.S. Workplace, 1960-1985." *Industrial and Labor Relations Review.* 44: 486-502.

Hughes, Katherine L., David Thornton Moore, Thomas R. Bailey. 1999. "Work-Based Learning and Academic Skills." Working Paper 15. Institute on Education and the Economy, Teachers College, Columbia University.

Hull, Glynda. 1991. "Hearing Other Voices: A Critical Assessment of Popular Views on Literacy and Work." Berkeley, CA.: National Center for Research in Vocational Education.

Hunt, Earl. 1995. *Will We Be Smart Enough: A Cognitive Analysis of the Coming Workforce*. New York: Russell Sage.

International Labor Office. 2001. *World Employment Report 2001: Life at Work in the Information Economy*. Geneva.

Jencks, Christopher. 1998. "Racial Bias in Testing." Pp.55-85 in *The Black-White Test Score Gap*, Christopher Jencks and Meredith Phillips eds. Washington, DC: Brookings.

Johnson, Rucker and Mary Corcoran. 2002. "Welfare Recipients' Road to Economic Self-Sufficiency: Job Quality and Job Transition Patterns Post-PRWORA." Manuscript. University of Michigan.

Johnston, William B, and Arnold E. Packer. 1987. *Workforce 2000: Work and Workers for the 21st Century*. Indianapolis, IN: Hudson Institute.

Jones, Lyle V. 1981. "Achievement Test Scores in Math and Science." *Science*. 213: 412-6.

Katz, Lawrence F. and Kevin M. Murphy. 1992. "Changes in Relative Wages, 1963-1987: Supply and Demand Factors." *Quarterly Journal of Economics*. 107: 35-78.

Katz, Lawrence F. and Lawrence H. Summers. 1989. "Industry Rents: Evidence and Implications." *Brookings Papers: Microeconomics*. 1989: 209-290.

Keep, Ewart and Ken Mayhew. 1996. "Evaluating the Assumptions that Underlie Training Policy." See Booth and Snower pp. 305-334.

Kelley, Catherine L. and Neil Charness. 1995. "Issues in Training Older Adults to Use Computers." *Behaviour and Information Technology*. 14: 107-20.

Kirsch, Irwin S. and Ann Jungeblut. 1986. "Literacy: Profiles of America's Young Adults." Princeton, NJ: Educational Testing Service.

Kirsch, Irwin S., Ann Jungeblut, Lynn Jenkins, and Andrew Kolstad. 1993. *Adult Literacy in America: A First Look at the Results of the National Adult Literacy Survey*. National Center for Education Statistics. Washington, DC: U.S. Department of Education.

Koretz, Daniel. 1986. "Trends in Educational Achievement." Washington, DC: Congressional Budget Office.

Koretz, Daniel. 1992. "What Happened to Test Scores, and Why?" *Educational Measurement: Issues and Practice*. Winter: 7-11.

Koretz, Daniel. 2000. "Limitations in the Use of Achievement Tests as Measures of Educators' Productivity." Manuscript.

Kozol, Jonathan. 1986. "Illiteracy Statistics: A Numbers Game." *New York Times*. October 30, 1986: A31.

Krahn, Harvey and Graham S. Lowe. 1998. "Literacy Utilization in Canadian Workplaces." Ottawa: Statistics Canada.

Lerman, Robert I. and Caroline Ratclife. 2001. "Are Single Mothers Finding Jobs Without Displacing Other Workers?" *Monthly Labor Review*. July: 3-12.

Levin, Henry M. 1998a. "Schools—Scapegoats or Saviors." *New Political Economy*. 3: 139-43.

Levin, Henry M. 1998b. "Educational Performance Standards and the Economy." *Educational Research*. May: 4-10.

Levin, Henry M. and Carolyn Kelley. 1994. "Can Education Do It Alone?" *Economics of Education Review*. 13: 97-108.

Levy, Frank and Richard Murnane. 1996. "With What Skills are Computers a Complement?" *American Economic Review: Papers and Proceedings*. 86: 258-62.

Linn, Robert L., Daniel Koretz, and Eva L. Baker. 1996. "Assessing the Validity of the National Assessment of Educational Progress." Center for the Study of Evaluation. National Center for Research on Evaluation, Standards, and Student Testing. UCLA. Technical Report 416.

Mare, Robert D. 1995. "Changes in Educational Attainment and School Enrollment." pp. 155-213 in *State of the Union: America in the 1990s*, Reynolds Farley, ed. New York: Russell Sage Foundation.

Mathews, Jay. 2001. "Millions of Adults Illiterate No More; Director Revises Widely Quoted 1993 Study That Said 1 in 5 Couldn't Read." *Washington Post*. July 17, 2001: A9.

Maume, David J., Jr., A. Silvia Cancio, and T. David Evans. 1996. "Cognitive Skills and Racial Wage Inequality: Reply to Farkas and Vicknair." *American Sociological Review*. 61: 561-64.

Mikulecky, Larry. 1982. "Job Literacy: The Relationship Between School Preparation and Workplace Actuality." *Reading Research Quarterly*. 17: 400-19.

Mishel, Lawrence and Ruy A. Teixeira. 1991. *The Myth of the Coming Labor Shortage: Jobs, Skills, and Incomes of America's Workforce 2000*. Washington, DC: Economic Policy Institute.

Moffitt, Robert A. 2002. *From Welfare to Work: What the Evidence Shows*. Poverty Brief 13. Washington, DC: Brookings Institution.

Moss, Philip and Chris Tilly. 2001. *Stories Employers Tell: Race, Skill, and Hiring in America*. New York: Russell Sage.

Murnane, Richard J. and Frank Levy. 1996. *Teaching the New Basic Skills*. NY: Free Press.

Murnane, Richard J., John B. Willett, and Frank Levy. 1995. "The Growing Importance of Cognitive Skills in Wage Determination." *Review of Economics and Statistics*. 77: 251-66.

Murnane, Richard J., John B. Willett, Margaret Jay Braatz, and Yves Duhaldeborde. 2001. "Do Different Dimensions of Male High School Students' Skills Predict Labor Market Success a Decade Later? Evidence from the NLSY." *Economics of Education Review*. 20: 311-20.

Murphy, Kevin M. and Finis Welch. 1993. "Occupational Change and the Demand for Skill, 1940-1990." *American Economic Review: Papers and Proceedings.* 83: 122-26.

National Association of Manufacturers. 2001. "The Skills Gap." Washington, DC: National Association of Manufacturers.

National Center on the Educational Quality of the Workforce. 1994. "The EQW National Employer Survey: First Findings." Philadelphia, PA: National Center on the Educational Quality of the Workforce.

National Commission on Writing in America's Schools and Colleges. 2003. "The Neglected "R": The Need for a Writing Revolution." New York: The College Board.

National Research Council. 1999. *The Changing Nature of Work: Implications for Occupational Analysis.* Washington, DC: National Academy Press.

National Research Council. 2001. *Building a Workforce for the Information Economy.* Washington, DC: National Academy Press.

Neal, Derek A. and William R. Johnson. 1996. "The Role of Premarket Factors in Black-White Wage Differences." *Journal of Political Economy.* 104: 869-95.

Neisser, Ulrich, ed. 1998. *The Rising Curve: Long-Term Gains in IQ and Related Measures.* Washington, DC: American Psychological Association.

Organization for Economic Cooperation and Development. 2001. *Knowledge and Skills for Life: First Results from the OECD Programme for International Student Assessment (PISA) 2000.* Paris.

Organization for Economic Cooperation and Development and Statistics Canada. 2000. *Literacy in the Information Age: Final Report of the International Adult Literacy Survey.* Paris.

O'Neil, Harold F. Jr., Keith Allred, Eva L. Baker. 1992. "Measurement of Workforce Readiness: Review of Theoretical Frameworks." National Center for Research on Evaluation, Standards, and Student Testing, Graduate School of Education, University of California, Los Angeles.

Ono, Yumiko. 2002. "Rethinking How Japanese Should Think." *Wall Street Journal.* March 25, 2002: 12

Payne, Jonathan. 1999. "All Things To All People: Changing Perceptions of 'Skill' Among Britain's Policy Makers Since the 1950s and Their Implications." SKOPE Research Paper No. 1. Oxford University.

Pearlman, Kenneth. 1997. "Twenty-First Century Measures for Twenty-First Century Work." Pp.136-179 in *Transitions in Work and Learning*, Alan Lesgold, Michael J. Foster, and Allison M. Black eds. Washington, DC: National Academy Press.

Pellegrino, James W., Lee R. Jones, and Karen J. Mitchell. 1999. *Grading the Nation's Report Card.* Washington, DC: National Academy Press

Peterson, Paul E. 2003. "Little Gain in Student Achievement." pp.39-72 in *Our Schools and Our Future*, Paul E. Peterson ed. Stanford, CA: Hoover Institution Press.

Public Agenda. 1999. "Reality Check: The Status of Standards Reform." http://www.publicagenda.org/specials/rcheck/rcheck1d.htm.

Reich, Robert B. 1991. *The Work of Nations.* New York: A. A. Knopf.

Reston, James. 1986. "Washington, Read It If You Can." *New York Times.* September 28, 1986: 25.

Robinson, Peter. 1998. "Literacy, Numeracy, and Economic Performance." *New Political Economy.* 3: 143-9.

Rosenbaum, James, Amy Binder. 1997. "Do Employers Really Need More Educated Youth?" *Sociology of Education.* 70: 68-85.

Rothstein, Richard. 2001. "Doubling of A's at Harvard: Grade Inflation or Brains?" *New York Times.* December 5, 2001: D8

Schmidt, Frank L. and John E. Hunter. 1998. "The Validity and Utility Inequality Selection Methods in Personnel Psychology: Practical and Theoretical Implications of 85 Years of Research Findings." *Psychological Bulletin.* 124: 262-74.

Schmidt, Stephanie R. 1999. "Long-Run Trends in Workers' Beliefs about Their Own Job Security: Evidence from the General Social Survey." *Journal of Labor Economics.* 17: S127-S141.

Schooler, Carmi. 1998. "Environmental Complexity and the Flynn Effect." See Neisser 1998, pp. 67-79.

Scribner, Sylvia. "Thinking in Action: Some Characteristics of Practical Thought." See Sternberg and Wagner, pp.13-30.

Sicherman, Nachum. 1991. "Overeducation in the Labor Market." *Journal Labor Economics.* 9: 101-22.

Smith, John P. III. 1999. "Tracking the Mathematics of Automobile Production: Are Schools Failing to Prepare Students for Work?" *American Educational Research Journal.* 36: 835-78.

Smith, M. Cecil. 1995. "Differences in Adults' Reading Practices and Literacy Proficiencies." *Reading Research Quarterly.* 31: 196-219.

Smith, Vicki. 1997. "New Forms of Work Organization." *Annual Review of Sociology.* 23: 315-39.

Spenner, Kenneth I. 1979. "Temporal Change in Work Content." *Annual Review of Sociology.* 44: 968-75.

Spenner, Kenneth I. 1988. "Technological Changes, Skill Requirements, and Education: The Case for Uncertainty." Pp. 131-84 in *The Impact of Technological Change on Employment and Economic Growth*, Richard M. Cyert and David Mowery, eds. Cambridge, MA: Ballinger.

Spenner, Kenneth I. 1990. "Skill: *Meanings, Methods, and Measures.*" *Work and Occupations.* 17: 399-421.

Stasz, Catherine. 2001. "Assessing Skills for Work: Two Perspectives." *Oxford Economic Papers.* 53: 385-405.

Stedman, Lawrence C. and Carl F. Kaestle. 1991. Literacy and reading performance in the United States from 1880 to the present. pp. 75-128 in *Literacy in the United States: Readers and Reading Since 1880*, Carl F. Kaestle et al. New Haven: Yale University Press.

Sternberg, Robert J. and Richard K. Wagner. 1986. *Practical Intelligence: Nature and Origins of Competence in the Everyday World*. London: Cambridge University Press.

Sticht, Thomas G. 1992. "Military Testing and Public Policy: Selected Studies of Lower Aptitude Personnel." pp.1-77 in *Test Policy in Defense: Lessons from the Military for Education, Training, and Employment*, Bernard R. Gifford and Linda C. Wing, eds. Boston: Kluwer Academic Publishers.

Sum, Andrew M. 1999. *Literacy in the Labor Force*. National Center for Education Statistics. Washington, DC: U.S. Department of Education.

Sum, Andrew M., Irwin S. Kirsch, and Robert Taggart. 2002. "The Twin Challenges of Mediocrity and Inequality: Literacy in the U.S. from an International Perspective. Princeton, NJ: Educational Testing Service.

Tam, Tony. 1997. "Sex Segregation and Occupational Gender Inequality in the United States: Devaluation or Specialized Training?" *American Journal of Sociology*. 102: 1652-92.

Teixeira, Ruy. 1998. "Rural and Urban Manufacturing Workers: Similar Problems, Similar Challenges." U.S. Department of Agriculture: Information Bulletin Number 736-02 (January).

Tyler, John, Richard J. Murnane, and Frank Levy. 1995. "Are More College Graduates Really Taking 'High School' Jobs?" *Monthly Labor Review*. Dec: 18-27.

Thurow, Lester C. 1975. *Generating Inequality: Mechanisms of Distribution in the U.S. Economy*. New York: Basic Books.

U.S. Congress. Office of Technology Assessment. 1990. *Worker Training: Competing in the New International Economy*. Washington, DC: Government Printing Office.

U.S. Department of Education. National Center for Education Statistics. 1998. "Developing the National Assessment of Adult Literacy: Recommendations from Stakeholders." Working paper No. 98-17 by Renee Sherman, Larry Condelli, and Judy Koloski. Washington, DC.

U.S. Department of Education. National Center for Education Statistics. 2000. "'How Much Literacy is Enough?' Issues in Defining and Reporting Performance Standards for the National Assessment of Adult Literacy." Working paper No. 2000-07 by Regie Stites. Washington, DC.

U.S. Department of Education. National Center for Education Statistics. 2001. *Digest of Education Statistics*. Washington, DC: GPO.

U.S. Department of Health, Education, and Welfare. 1973. *Work in America*. Cambridge, MA: MIT Press.

U.S. Department of Labor. Bureau of Labor Statistics. 1992. *How Workers Get Their Training: A 1991 Update*. Bulletin 2407.

U.S. Department of Labor. Secretary's Commission on Achieving Necessary Skills. 1991. *What Work Requires of Schools: A SCANS Report for America 2000*. Washington, DC.

U.S. National Commission on Excellence in Education. 1983. *A Nation at Risk: The Imperative for Educational Reform*. Washington, DC: Government Printing Office.

Weakliem David, Julia McQuillan, and Terry Schauer. 1995. "Toward Meritocracy? Changing Social-Class Differences in Intellectual Ability." *Sociology of Education*. 68: 271-86.

Westerman SJ, Davies DR, Glendon AI, Stammers RB, Matthews G. 1995. Age and cognitive ability as predictors of computerized information retrieval. *Behaviour and Information Technology*. 14: 313–26.

Williams, Wendy M. and Stephen J. Ceci. 1997. "Are Americans becoming more or less alike?: Trends in race, class, and ability differences in intelligence. *American Psychology*. 52: 1226-35.

Wilson, James A. and Walter R. Gove. 1999a. "The Intercohort Decline in Verbal Ability: Does It Exist?" *American Sociological Review*. 67: 253-66.

Wilson, James A. and Walter R. Gove. 1999b. Reply: "The Age-Period-Cohort Conundrum and Verbal Ability." *American Sociological Review*. 67: 287-302.

Wilson, William J. 1987. *The Truly Disadvantaged*. Chicago: University of Chicago Press.

Wilson, William J. 1996. *When Work Disappears: The World of the New Urban Poor*. New York: Knopf.

Winerip, Michael. 1994. "S.A.T. Increases the Average Score, By Fiat." *New York Times*. June 11, 1994: 1.

Woodward, Joan. 1965. *Industrial Organization*. London: Oxford University Press.

Wright, Erik Olin and Bill Martin. 1987. "The Transformation of the American Class Structure, 1960-1980." *American Journal of Sociology*. 93: 1-29.

Zemsky, Robert. 1997. "Skills and the Economy: An Employer Context for Understanding the School-to-Work Transition." pp.34-61 in *Transitions in Work and Learning*, Alan Lesgold, Michael J. Foster, and Allison M. Black eds. Washington, DC: National Academy Press.

Zuboff, Shoshana. 1988. *In the Age of the Smart Machine: The Future of Work and Power*. New York: Basic Books.

About EPI

The Economic Policy Institute was founded in 1986 to widen the debate about policies to achieve healthy economic growth, prosperity, and opportunity.

In the United States today, inequality in wealth, wages, and income remains historically high. Expanding global competition, changes in the nature of work, and rapid technological advances are altering economic reality. Yet many of our policies, attitudes, and institutions are based on assumptions that no longer reflect real world conditions.

With the support of leaders from labor, business, and the foundation world, the Institute has sponsored research and public discussion of a wide variety of topics: trade and fiscal policies; trends in wages, incomes, and prices; education; the causes of the productivity slowdown; labor market problems; rural and urban policies; inflation; state-level economic development strategies; comparative international economic performance; and studies of the overall health of the U.S. manufacturing sector and of specific key industries.

The Institute works with a growing network of innovative economists and other social science researchers in universities and research centers in the U.S. and abroad who are willing to go beyond the conventional wisdom in considering strategies for public policy.

Founding scholars of the Institute include Jeff Faux, distinguished fellow and former president of EPI; Lester Thurow, Sloan School of Management, MIT; Ray Marshall, former U.S. secretary of labor, professor at the LBJ School of Public Affairs, University of Texas; Barry Bluestone, Northeastern University; Robert Reich, former U.S. secretary of labor; and Robert Kuttner, author, editor of *The American Prospect,* and columnist for *Business Week* and the Washington Post Writers Group.

For additional information about the Institute, contact EPI at 1660 L Street NW, Suite 1200, Washington, DC 20036, (202) 775-8810, or visit www.epinet.org.